NEW SPA FOOD

Hearty, healthy recipes, from the Norwich Inn and Spa

NEW SPA FOOD

EDWARD J. SAFDIE

PHOTOGRAPHS BY MARIA ROBLEDO

TEXT BY JUDY KNIPE

PRODUCED BY CARLENE SAFDIE
STYLING BY ANITA CALERO
FOOD STYLING BY JOHN ROBERT MASSIE

Clarkson N. Potter, Inc./Publishers, New York

To Jack and Jean Safdie,
my mother and father
E. J. S.

Designed by Dania Martinez Davey

**Readers are advised to consult with their doctors
or nutritionists before undertaking any dietary program.**

**Spa Food is a trademark of Edward J. Safdie.
For further information on the Norwich Inn and Spa and their programs,
please contact: The Norwich Inn, Spa, and Villas
Route 32
Norwich, CT 06360
(203) 886-2401**

Published by Clarkson N. Potter, Inc.,
201 East 50th Street, New York, New York 10022
CLARKSON N. POTTER, POTTER, and colophon are trademarks of
Clarkson N. Potter, Inc.

Printed in Japan

Library of Congress Cataloging-in-Publication Data
Safdie, Edward J.
New spa food: hearty, healthy recipes from the Norwich Inn and Spa
/by Edward J. Safdie; photographs by Maria Robledo; text by Judy
Knipe.—1st ed.
p. cm.
1. Low-calorie diet—Recipes. I. Knipe, Judy. II. Title.
RM222.2.S214 1990
641.5′63—dc20   90–31348
ISBN 0-517-57534-5
10 9 8 7 6 5 4 3 2 1
First Edition

c o n t e n t s

d u c t i o n

Over the last two decades, I've owned and developed spas in Europe, the Southwest, California, and our latest Inn and Spa in New England's historic Norwich, Connecticut. While the specifics of the Spa program have been formulated individually at each one, we've always taken a "real life" approach to the spa experience, foregoing a clinical setting in favor of one that more closely approximates the environment in which people must live once they leave the Spa behind. Rather than segregating Spa guests from visitors to the inns, which would effectively shield them from the temptations of eating with others not on a restricted diet, we encourage both groups to mingle, to take meals together and make use of our exercise and treatment facilities. I've always felt that it's easy to eat well (and sparingly) under the watchful eye of a nutritionist, especially when you are surrounded by others on precisely the same regimen. But once that close supervision ends, people invariably revert to their previous ways of living and eating, undoing all the good they accomplished during their stay. I knew that to help our Spa guests establish eating and cooking habits that would last a lifetime, we had to develop a program they could really live with.

And that's exactly what New Spa Food is. Not a weight-loss program per se, or even a "diet," New Spa Food is simply a *better* way to eat that will result in healthy, gradual weight loss when combined with a sensible program of exercise. Low in cholesterol, sodium, saturated fats, and, of course, calories, this is a cuisine based on fresh fruits, grains, and lean meats that is both wholesome and, most important, satisfying, and that incorporates much of the medical evidence that has come to light about cholesterol, heart disease, and food additives. It's the way we think *everyone* will be eating in the century to come.

When we first introduced Spa food, it was a revelation to dieters, who had come to expect nothing but "rabbit food" from a spa regimen. Today the term "spa food" is so commonplace that it barely raises an eyebrow on menus from four-star restaurants right down to fast-food chains. My first book, *Spa Food,* which was based on the menus at my California Spa, is on the list of recommended reading at the Cornell University hotel school, and I've heard that a prominent New York physician has been known to hand a copy of the book to his overweight patients. I even noted a recent article in which a young married couple told of having given the book to the caterer who was to prepare their wedding feast. In short, people were clearly ready for our message that healthful, low-calorie food could be delicious and beautiful to look at, and they embraced our philosophy eagerly.

But the evolution of the Spa philosophy continued. Since the publication of *Spa Food,* attitudes have changed, and our approach toward health and beauty has relaxed some-what. That old bromide "You can't be too rich or too thin" no longer holds; most of us have accepted the fact that you don't have to be rail-thin to be attractive. It's not only medically unsound to practice the relentless self-denial needed to maintain what may be an unnaturally low weight, it's become socially unacceptable to do so.

Today people are no longer willing to deny themselves the pleasure of hearty, homey, abundant meals. And while many of our Spa guests still enjoy using the original *Spa Food* regimen as a cleansing diet, to counteract the effects of an overly indulgent week or two, or as an effective way to jump-start a new diet program, they find that it dovetails nicely with the more moderate approach to diet and health we espouse at the Spa today.

Today flexibility and a return to basics are the cornerstones of our "real life" approach at The Norwich Inn and Spa in Connecticut. That approach starts with the structure of the Spa program itself. While we still offer our traditional five-day Spa program, we've added a roster of one-, two-, and three-day "revitalizer" and "energizer" programs that allow guests to tailor an exercise, diet, and beauty program to their own needs. And I've been delighted to see that it's not only our Spa guests who take advantage of these programs. Michael Douglas visited the Inn and set a Spa record on the rowing machine, maintaining an Olympic single scull pace for 17 minutes! Debra Winger, a swimming enthusiast, made use of the pool during her visit, and such guests as Joan Rivers, Mario Buatta, Bill and Pat Buckley, Placido Domingo, Carly Simon, and super models Cheryl Tiegs and Elle Macpherson have all integrated elements of the Spa program into their stays at the Inn.

And just like the Spa program, flexibility is the keynote of New Spa Food. The Spa meal plans offer a number of options that can be adapted to individual tastes and requirements. Norwich, Connecticut, is in the heart of New England, a region with its own longstanding culinary tradition of hearty, healthful food, and we've made that tradition the foundation of the New Spa Food programs. We've developed a 1,250-calorie-a-day weight-loss menu, a 1,550-calorie maintenance program that we call Yankee Ingenuity, and eight special-occasion menus that are abundant and festive, yet true to the tenets of New Spa cooking. And even within these categories dishes can be added or substituted, portions altered, or seasonings changed to fit your preferences and needs.

Except for such high-cholesterol items as heavy cream, or foods tainted with additives or preservatives, nothing is excluded from this diet, not even alcoholic beverages (in moderation). We believe that an occasional glass of fine vintage wine, a sparkling spritzer, or low-alcohol beer enhances the meal and lifts one's spirits. And because nothing can replace the rich flavor of real butter, we've used it, with restraint, in certain recipes. Of course, we've also found new ways to use grains, low-fat dairy products, lean meats, and fresh herbs that result in meals so flavorful and satisfying that no one misses the caloric, high-cholesterol ingredients we left out.

Best of all, our experience has shown that our New Spa Food is still a very effective part of a weight-loss program when used in conjunction with a program of exercise. Most of our guests lose up to five pounds after a week on this plan, without any feeling of deprivation. In fact, many say they find our portions *too* generous! The response to our new Spa menus has been so enthusiastic that we now offer Spa dishes on our Norwich Inn restaurant menu, and they find as many devotees among our regular restaurant customers as among Spa guests, because no one today can afford to be unconcerned about healthier eating.

My father and mother, like most parents, always wanted their children to be "healthy, wealthy, and wise." But of all of these, they maintained, health is the most important, because without your health, the other two won't do you much good. I couldn't agree more, and that's why it was so important to me that New Spa Food feed the soul as well as the body. We think of it as food for a lifetime, and we hope you will, too.

the spa

program

1250
CALORIE MENUS

Before we began developing menus for the New Spa Food weight-loss program, our chef, Daniel Kucharski, and I consulted with nutritionists and our health professionals to arrive at a meaningful daily calorie count, one that would amply satisfy the appetite while allowing a dieter who exercised regularly to lose weight. The experts' recommendations and the input we'd had from Spa guests convinced us that, for women, about 1,250 calories a day was a realistic goal. People who take in less than 1,250 calories for longer than a week are hungry all the time; they enter a kind of "deprivation zone," and, as we know by now, deprivation leads to bingeing, which can trigger an unhealthy cycle of overeating and guilt.

It's important to remember, however, that 1,250 is not a magic number. For most men and some women this may not be enough calories. If you feel hungry and tired after following this program for two or three days, or if you already know that you enter your deprivation zone at a level in excess of 1,250 calories, you can always *add* extra calories in the form of fruits, vegetables, pasta, and other grains. Some, on the other hand, may find 1,250 calories a day too many, even for maintenance, or simply feel that the portions offered in the program leave them too full. If this is true for you, cut down on portion sizes, skip a dessert now and then, or leave some food on your plate—an extraordinary luxury for someone on a diet plan—and exercise more to lose at the rate you desire.

Once we had established the calorie count, we spent many hours tossing around ideas about what *we* liked to eat and how these foods could be integrated into a spa program. We tested and tasted hundreds of dishes, and asked our guests what they thought of those that met our rigorous standards. We were fascinated to see that, overwhelmingly, our guests preferred food that was comforting and familiar, food they could eat and serve in the real world, where other people's needs and preferences also had to be considered. These tastes coincided with our own, and that's why most of the recipes in the Spa program, and in this book, are delicious American home cooking—but with less calories, fat, sodium, and cholesterol.

There are several important principles we follow in planning menus and recipes:

• The first is a sensible distribution of calories among the three main nutrient groups. Although the exact figures vary from day to day, we try to allocate 55 to 60 percent of each day's calories to carbohydrates, 30 percent or less to fats, and the remainder to protein. These strictures, to which we adhere closely but not slavishly, are in line with recommendations from the U.S. government, the American Heart Association, and the American Diabetes Association.

• Whole grains and other high-fiber carbohydrates are the bedrock of the Spa meal program. Potatoes, bran and oat bran muffins, whole wheat and buckwheat pastas, bulgur, couscous, and stone-ground whole wheat bread—one of these is included in every meal.

• Foods high in cholesterol are severely restricted. For instance, we make our omelets and scrambled eggs with only one whole egg and two egg whites, and egg whites are frequently substituted for whole eggs in muffin and custard recipes. It's true that we use butter, but in very small amounts and in only two or three recipes. For nearly everything else, we use olive oil, a delicious monounsaturated fat, and polyunsaturated fats such as corn oil and cold-pressed safflower oil, all of which help to lower serum cholesterol. When sautéing vegetables and poultry, sometimes we dispense with fats altogether by using nonstick skillets sprayed with vegetable cooking spray.

• Fresh fish and shellfish are served at least three times a week at the Spa, and we provide seafood entrées for those of our guests who eat no poultry or red meat. Veal, chicken, and turkey appear in moderate amounts.

• Spa guests eat one vegetarian lunch or dinner every day, with main courses as diverse as hearty soups, braised vegetables, and whole-grain salads.

• We offer a dessert with every lunch and dinner, usually one based on fresh fruit made into a prepared dessert, such as ice cream or compote.

It's quite likely that at some point during the year you'll feel the need to trim down and lose the weight you gained over the holidays or on a vacation. If you can get away to a spa, so much the better. If you can't, we urge you to try the Norwich Spa weight-loss program at home. Start by consulting your doctor; be sure to exercise sensibly and regularly, and, for one or two weeks, follow the menus and recipes that begin on the next page. Then, using our New Spa Food nutritional principles as guidelines, you can devise your own program and stay on it for as long as you must to lose the weight you want to take off at whatever rate you are comfortable with.

Bear in mind, however, that rigid adherence to any diet is self-defeating. It's okay to allow yourself an occasional extravagance—an extra slice of toast at breakfast once or twice a week, unbuttered popcorn at the movies now and then (bring a small shaker of vegetable seasoning from home to give it some punch) or a toasted pita or crispy flatbread for an afternoon snack. Your body will be able to cope with these added calories, and you'll continue to lose weight, especially if you stay active and don't fall into the pit of self-recrimination, which leads to overindulgence.

Instead, be flexible, be good to yourself, and enjoy every bite.

D A Y

1

B R E A K F A S T

250
CALORIES

•

HOT OAT BRAN CEREAL
WITH FRUIT AND HOT MILK

•

DECAFFEINATED COFFEE OR TEA

•

L U N C H

319
CALORIES

•

SPINACH PIE WITH
WHOLE-GRAIN MUSTARD SAUCE

•

RADICCHIO AND WATERCRESS
SALAD

•

FRESH HERB DRESSING

•

PINEAPPLE-BANANA SORBET

•

HOT OAT BRAN CEREAL WITH FRUIT AND HOT MILK

250
CALORIES PER SERVING

Hot oat bran cereal may be good for you but, let's face it, "bland" is the word that best describes it. To give your breakfast a little crunch, sprinkle the oat bran with a spoonful or two of crisp dry cereal, such as Grapenuts, toasted rolled oats, or Puffed Kashi, and some berries—the seeds add texture and fiber. When you buy oat bran cereal be sure it contains no added sugar or salt.

1⅓ cups raw oat bran cereal
1 quart water
½ cup Grapenuts cereal
2 cups berries (raspberries, blackberries, blueberries, or quartered strawberries)
4 teaspoons maple syrup
2 cups skim milk, heated

Combine the oat bran cereal and water in a medium saucepan and stir to mix well. Bring to a boil over high heat, reduce the heat, and simmer for 1 minute, stirring 2 or 3 times.

Divide the oat bran among 4 cereal bowls. Sprinkle with the Grapenuts and then the berries. Drizzle 1 teaspoon of maple syrup over each serving. Serve the milk in a pitcher.

Serves 4

SPINACH PIE WITH WHOLE-GRAIN MUSTARD SAUCE

180
CALORIES PER SERVING

Filo, the wonderfully flaky Greek pastry dough that's so difficult to prepare by hand and so convenient to buy in packages, can be relatively low in calories when it's used as we do at the Spa. Instead of brushing each layer with melted butter, we spray the sheets with vegetable cooking spray. Using filo in innovative ways is a Spa specialty, and this virtually fatless rendition of traditional Greek spanakopita is a good example. You can make 4 large pies or 8 smaller ones, serving 2 per person.

FILLING

1 pound spinach
2 leeks (white part only)
2 tablespoons minced shallots
1 tablespoon minced garlic
¼ cup dry white wine
3 medium tomatoes
1 cup sliced mushrooms
¼ teaspoon freshly grated nutmeg
Freshly ground white pepper
Vegetable seasoning

4 sheets filo dough

SAUCE

1 cup plain low-fat or nonfat yogurt
4 teaspoons whole-grain mustard

Trim the stalks from the spinach and wash the leaves thoroughly. Drain and set aside.

Trim the leeks, wash thoroughly, and slice them thin. Put the leeks, shallots, garlic, and wine in a medium saucepan and cook over medium heat, stirring occasionally, until the vegetables are translucent and the wine has evaporated, about 6 minutes.

Core and chop the tomatoes; you should have about 4 cups. Add the tomatoes and mushrooms to the leek mixture and cook 5 minutes longer. Add the spinach and cook, stirring often, until it is wilted, 2 to 3 minutes. Add the nutmeg and pepper, and vegetable seasoning to taste. Spread the filling on a platter or baking sheet to cool.

Preheat the oven to 350° F. Line a baking sheet with parchment paper. Place the sheets of filo on a work surface, edges lined up, and cover with a damp cloth.

Remove 1 sheet of filo and spray it lightly with vegetable cooking spray. Divide the filling into 8 portions and center 1 portion about 2 inches from the bottom of the filo sheet. Fold up the lower left corner of the filo over the filling, so that the bottom of the filo aligns with the right edge, forming a triangle over the filling. Fold the filling straight along the top of the triangle, so that it aligns with the left edge of the sheet. Continue folding up and right, up and left, until you reach the end of the sheet of dough. Place the packet seam side down on the prepared baking sheet. Make 7 more pies, arrange them on the baking sheet, and spray with vegetable cooking spray. Bake the pies until they are golden brown, about 20 to 25 minutes.

Just before serving, make the sauce. In a small saucepan whisk together the yogurt and mustard and place over low heat just until lukewarm, 2 to 3 minutes. Do not allow the sauce to become too hot or the yogurt will separate.

Spoon ¼ cup of sauce onto 4 warm plates, place the spinach pies on top of the sauce, and serve at once.

Serves 4

RADICCHIO AND WATERCRESS SALAD

35
CALORIES PER SERVING

Radicchio and watercress are an attractive couple, but any other greens you find appealing will do just as nicely. Toss the salad very well to distribute the dressing thoroughly. Hands work best, but if that strikes you as too messy, use 2 spoons instead.

8 large radicchio leaves
2 bunches watercress
¼ cup Fresh Herb Dressing

Tear the radicchio into bite-size pieces. Discard the thick watercress stems, rinse, and pat dry. Place the radicchio and watercress in a bowl and, just before serving, toss with the dressing.

Serves 4

FRESH HERB DRESSING

30
CALORIES PER TABLESPOON

A profusion of fresh herbs can now be found throughout the year, even in supermarkets. Here, lemon thyme, basil, chives, and tarragon are teamed with balsamic vinegar and a fine olive oil, but feel free to devise your own blend with herbs from your garden or whatever is freshest at the market.

¼ cup balsamic vinegar
½ cup extra-virgin olive oil
1½ cups sparkling mineral water
** or seltzer**
2 garlic cloves gently crushed with
** the flat of a knife**
¼ cup loosely packed fresh lemon
** thyme leaves**
¼ cup loosely packed chopped
** fresh basil**
¼ cup loosely packed snipped
** fresh chives**
⅛ cup loosely packed chopped
** fresh tarragon**
Freshly ground white pepper

In a blender or food processor, combine the vinegar and oil and process until well blended. Pour the mixture into a bowl, stir in the mineral water, garlic, thyme, basil, chives, tarragon, and a pinch of pepper, and cover with plastic wrap. Store in the refrigerator for up to 3 days.

Makes 2½ cups

PINEAPPLE-BANANA SORBET

104
CALORIES PER SERVING

A little bit of tropical paradise. Perfectly ripe pineapple needs no added sugar, just a little naturally sweet apple juice to help to make a smooth puree. A few strawberries pureed with the pineapple and bananas will tint the sorbet pink. Try a scoop in a glass of sparkling water (flavored if you like) for a zingy tropical float.

1 pineapple
2 bananas
¼ cup apple juice

Cut off the top of the pineapple, then cut away the rind and eyes. Halve the fruit lengthwise, remove the core, and cut the pineapple into chunks over a bowl to catch any juice. Place the pineapple, with its juice, in the bowl of a food processor fitted with the steel blade. Peel the bananas, cut them into thick slices, and add to the food processor. Process until the fruit is pureed, then add the apple juice and process again until the mixture is very smooth.

Turn the mixture into an electric or hand-cranked ice-cream maker and freeze, following the manufacturer's instructions. To make the sorbet in your freezer, transfer the mixture to a bowl and place in the freezer. When the liquid has frozen solid, about 2 to 3 hours, remove it from the freezer and with a fork, break it into large chunks. Place the chunks in a food processor and process with the steel blade until smooth and creamy. Return it to the bowl and freeze for at least 30 minutes. Serve in chilled dessert dishes.

Serves 4 to 6

D A Y
1

D I N N E R

560
CALORIES

•

SPRIGHTLY SPRITZER

•

NORWICH INN NEW ENGLAND
BOILED DINNER

•

GREEN SAUCE OR FRESH
HORSERADISH SAUCE

•

MELBA MERINGUES

•

SPRIGHTLY SPRITZER

0

CALORIES PER SERVING

By now the classic mineral water spritzer —sparkling water with a twist of lemon or lime—raises few eyebrows served in place of wine with even the most elegant meals. The lively carbonation and crisp citrus tang seem to complement most foods without adding a single calorie to the menu.

If, however, you want to expand your repertoire of spritzers, experiment with the wide variety of imported and domestic bottled waters, adding flavor with just a teaspoon or so of:

- Italian fruit syrups
- fruit liqueurs, such as créme de cassis
- bottled extracts
- herbal infusions, such as lavender

Or try this slightly more elaborate concoction that tastes like an alcoholic beverage, although it contains none and has only 4 calories per serving.

ROSE GERANIUM COCKTAIL

2½ cups cold tap water
4 tea bags (orange pekoe or rose hip are best)
6 rose geranium leaves (*pelargonium graveolens*)
12 whole cloves
2 quarts sparkling mineral water

Combine the tap water, tea bags, rose geranium leaves, and cloves in a small saucepan and bring to a simmer. Cook for 10 minutes, then strain and allow to cool. Stir in the mineral water. Serve over ice in tall glasses.

Serves 4

NORWICH INN NEW ENGLAND BOILED DINNER

360

CALORIES PER SERVING

We offer this adaptation of a New England classic on the Spa and regular menus at the Norwich Inn. Instead of the usual cholesterol-rich brisket of beef, chicken breasts simmer with vegetables in homemade stock. And because everything cooks in one pot, it's a simple, soothing dish for a cool fall evening. Garlic and tomatoes add a hint of the Mediterranean, as does the green sauce. At the Spa, we use chicken breasts with the bone still in and the first wing joint attached, but ordinary chicken breast halves are just fine.

2 garlic cloves
2 leeks (white part only)
3 celery stalks
2 carrots
½ head green cabbage
4 medium Red Bliss potatoes
2 tomatoes
4 chicken breast halves, skin removed (with wing joint, if desired)
½ cup dry white wine
1 teaspoon caraway seeds
2 teaspoons chopped fresh tarragon or 1 teaspoon dried
1 bay leaf
6 cups Low-Sodium Chicken Stock (page 141)
Chopped Italian parsley

Crush the garlic with the flat side of a knife and pull off and discard the skin. Wash the leeks well and cut into 1-inch lengths. Trim the celery and cut into 1-inch lengths. Peel and quarter the carrots and cut into 3-inch lengths. Cut the cabbage into 8 wedges and remove the core. With a vegetable peeler, remove the strip of peel from the center of each potato. Place the potatoes in a bowl of cold water to prevent them from darkening. Peel, seed, and roughly chop the tomatoes.

Spray a 4- or 5-quart Dutch oven with vegetable cooking spray and place over moderate heat. Add the chicken and sauté until lightly browned on both sides, about 5 to 7 minutes in all. Add the wine, garlic, leeks, and celery, and cook 5 minutes more. Add the carrots, cabbage, potatoes, tomatoes, caraway seeds, tarragon, bay leaf, and chicken stock, bring to a boil over high heat, then reduce the heat to moderately low. Cook, covered, until the vegetables are tender, about 30 minutes.

With a slotted spoon, transfer the chicken and vegetables to a warm tureen. Carefully pour over some of the hot broth.

Serve the chicken and vegetables with some of the broth in heated soup plates. Sprinkle with parsley. Serve with green sauce or fresh horseradish sauce.

Serves 4

GREEN SAUCE

9 0

CALORIES PER SERVING

An Italian condiment with a lively garlic flavor, green sauce is a combination of herbs, fruity olive oil, and vinegar that is often served with boiled meats and poultry.

2 tablespoons extra-virgin olive oil
1 tablespoon balsamic vinegar
2 garlic cloves
¼ cup chopped shallots
½ cup chopped celery
1 cup fresh basil leaves
1 cup Italian parsley leaves
Vegetable seasoning
Freshly ground black pepper

Place the oil, vinegar, garlic, shallots, celery, basil, parsley, and vegetable seasoning and black pepper to taste in a food processor fitted with the steel blade. Process to a paste and transfer to a serving bowl.

Serves 4

FRESH HORSERADISH SAUCE

2 6

CALORIES PER SERVING

Fresh horseradish root is often available at Oriental greengrocers and can be found in most supermarkets in springtime around the Passover holiday season. Homemade horseradish is wonderfully pungent, but remember that a little goes a long way. When you are peeling it, don't be surprised if your eyes water; horseradish is even stronger than onion. Although you will only need a small piece of the whole root for this recipe, the root, well wrapped in foil or plastic, keeps well in the vegetable bin of your refrigerator. Any leftover sauce can be served with cold boiled or roasted meats or in place of mayonnaise in tea sandwiches.

PREPARED HORSERADISH
1 ounce (approximately a 1-inch piece) fresh horseradish root
2 tablespoons cider vinegar
Pinch fructose

½ cup Norwich Spa Whipped Cream (page 23), made without fructose and vanilla extract

Peel the fresh horseradish root with a sharp paring knife or a vegetable peeler. Cut the root into quarters, place in the work bowl of a mini-food processor, and grate finely. Add the vinegar and fructose and process again until the mixture forms a very loose paste.

Place the whipped cream in a small bowl and fold in the prepared horseradish. Cover tightly and chill until serving time.

Serves 4

MELBA MERINGUES

1 1 0

CALORIES PER SERVING

Fresh peach halves, a ruby pool of pureed raspberries, capped with a lightly browned bonnet of meringue, are a joy to behold—and even better to eat.

1 pint fresh raspberries, or 1 10-ounce package frozen unsweetened raspberries, thawed
1 ripe banana, peeled and cut into chunks
2 peaches
Juice of 1 lemon
2 egg whites, at room temperature
1 tablespoon honey, warmed

Preheat the oven to 400° F. Spray a baking sheet with vegetable cooking spray.

In a food processor or blender, puree the berries and the banana. Strain the puree through a fine sieve and reserve. For a bit more texture, puree just half the fruit and stir in the remaining berries.

Bring a pot of water to a boil. With a long-handled fork, spear the peaches, one at a time, and submerge them in the boiling water for 10 seconds. Plunge the peaches into cold water, then slip off the skins. Halve the peaches, discard the pits, and place the fruit in a bowl of water acidulated with the lemon juice.

In a bowl, beat the egg whites until they hold firm peaks but are not dry. Drizzle in honey and beat until it is incorporated. Place the peach halves, cut side up, on the baking sheet and spoon one-quarter of the egg whites on each half, making decorative swirls. Bake for 4 to 5 minutes, or until the meringues are golden brown.

Divide the raspberry mixture among 4 serving plates. With a spatula, gently transfer a peach to each plate. Serve at once.

Serves 4

D A Y
2

B R E A K F A S T

260
CALORIES

•

WHOLE GRAIN TOAST
WITH FRUIT PRESERVES OR
FRUIT BUTTER

•

FRESH FRUIT WITH
COTTAGE CHEESE

•

DECAFFEINATED COFFEE OR TEA

•

LUNCH

385
CALORIES

•

WEISER BAKED POTATO WITH
MINI SALAD BAR

•

EXOTIC FRUIT SMOOTHIE

•

WHOLE GRAIN TOAST WITH FRUIT PRESERVES OR FRUIT BUTTER

120

CALORIES PER SERVING

Be sure to use the chewiest, heartiest stone-ground whole grain bread you can find. Fruit-only preserves are now commonly available in supermarkets or by mail direct from the orchards and growers themselves. But on days when you have a little extra time, or want to make breakfast a bit more special, try one of the many fruit butters we serve at the Spa. They have precious few calories and pack a big fruit taste that is delicious on breads, muffins—even scones, as we've served them in the tea on page 132.

4 slices chewy whole-grain bread
4 tablespoons fruit-only preserves or Apple Butter or Minted Pear Butter

Toast the bread and cut each slice into two pieces. Pass small bowls of the preserves or fruit butters separately.

Serves 4

MINTED PEAR BUTTER

29

CALORIES PER TABLESPOON

Your day will look brighter with your first taste of this minted honey-pear butter, which is especially good made with juicy Comice pears. Check the label on pear nectar to see that it's made with pear juice only. If your supermarket stocks nectar that contains high-fructose syrup, buy the nectar at a health-food store. You might want to vary the flavor of this spread by adding about a teaspoon of grated fresh ginger with the honey and lemon juice.

2½ cups canned or bottled pear nectar
2 or 3 fresh mint sprigs
4 large pears (Comice, Anjou, or Bosc)
¼ cup honey
Juice of ½ lemon
Fructose

Combine the pear nectar and mint in a heavy nonreactive saucepan, place over high heat, and bring to a boil. Boil the nectar, uncovered, until reduced by half, about 8 to 10 minutes. Discard the mint. While the nectar is being reduced, peel, core, and dice the pears.

When the nectar is reduced, add the honey, lemon juice, and fructose to taste and stir until they are dissolved. Add the pears and bring to a boil. Lower the heat and cook the mixture at a slow simmer, uncovered, until the pear butter is fairly thick, about 15 minutes, stirring often to keep it from sticking to the bottom of the pan.

Transfer the mixture to a blender or food processor fitted with the steel blade and puree. Store in the refrigerator in tightly covered containers for up to 3 weeks. Serve chilled.

Makes 1 pint

APPLE BUTTER

26

CALORIES PER TABLESPOON

For some, the fragrance of homemade apple butter simmering on the stove can summon up happy memories, and for everyone the aroma is the harbinger of a happy future spent eating this thick, spicy spread. Serve it with scones or toast.

2½ cups apple cider
3 large apples
¼ cup fructose
2 tablespoons honey
¼ teaspoon ground cinnamon or 1 cinnamon stick
1 whole clove
Pinch of ground allspice

Put the cider in a heavy, nonreactive saucepan, place over high heat, and bring to a boil. Boil the cider, uncovered, until it is reduced by half, about 8 to 10 minutes.

Meanwhile, peel, core, and slice the apples. Add them to the cider, reduce the heat, and simmer the mixture, uncovered, until mushy, about 10 minutes; stir frequently. Add the fructose, honey, cinnamon, clove, and allspice and continue to cook at a very slow simmer, uncovered, until the apple butter is fairly thick, about 20 minutes. Stir often to keep the mixture from sticking to the bottom of the pan.

Remove the cinnamon stick, if used, and puree the mixture in a blender or put through the fine blade of a food mill. Transfer the apple butter to a tightly covered container and store in the refrigerator for up to 3 weeks.

Makes 1 pint

FRESH FRUIT WITH COTTAGE CHEESE

140
CALORIES PER SERVING

This all-purpose breakfast can be made with any combination of seasonal fruits that pleases your palate. For this meal, we used strawberries, blueberries, raspberries, honeydew melon, and pineapple. To make it a bit more special, whip the cottage cheese in the blender for a smooth, creamy topping.

> 1⅓ cups 1% fat cottage cheese
> 4 cups fresh fruit, whole, sliced, or cubed
> Orange zest julienne (optional)

Divide the cottage cheese among 4 bowls, add the fruit, and decorate with the orange zest.

Serves 4

WEISER BAKED POTATO WITH MINI SALAD BAR

325
CALORIES PER SERVING

My wife, Carlene, who grew up in Idaho, claims Weiser's potatoes are the best. Blanched asparagus, broccoli, green beans, and cooked beets are all possible winning and decorative additions to this robust lunch, which gets a boost from a mustard- or soy-flavored yogurt. Be sure to eat the crisp skin, too!

> 4 medium baking potatoes
> 1 cup nonfat plain yogurt
> Dijon mustard or low-sodium soy sauce
> 12 large Boston lettuce leaves
> 12 radicchio leaves
> 1 cup mixed sprouts (lentil, sweet pea, adzuki, alfalfa, radish)
> 1 cup shredded carrots
> 1 cup shredded cheddar, Monterey Jack, or Asiago cheese
> 2 tablespoons raw sunflower seeds
> 1 cup mixed diced red, green, and yellow bell peppers
> Chopped fresh chives

Preheat the oven to 375° F. Bake the potatoes for 45 to 60 minutes, or until tender.

Meanwhile, combine the yogurt and mustard or soy sauce to taste. Arrange 3 leaves each of lettuce and radicchio around the edges of each dinner plate. Reserving ¼ cup of the yogurt mixture, fill 1 lettuce cup on each plate with a portion of sprouts, carrots, cheese, sunflower seeds, bell peppers, and the remaining yogurt mixture.

When the potatoes are tender, slice them open, place in the center of the plates, and spoon 1 tablespoon of the flavored yogurt over each. Top with chives.

Serves 4

EXOTIC FRUIT SMOOTHIE

60
CALORIES PER SERVING

Papaya nectar comes in cans or bottles and can be found at most supermarkets and health-food stores. Chill all the ingredients ahead of time, and make the dessert just before serving so it won't lose its frothy consistency.

> ½ cup chopped ice
> ½ cup papaya nectar
> 1 banana, cut into 1-inch pieces
> 1 cup fresh pineapple chunks
> ¼ cup raspberries
> 4 slices starfruit (optional)

Place the ice, papaya nectar, banana, pineapple, and raspberries in a blender and blend until smooth. Pour into glasses and garnish with the starfruit, if desired.

Serves 4

D A Y

2

D I N N E R

5 8 2
CALORIES

•

MIXED SEAFOOD GRILL

•

TOMATO GINGER COULIS

•

BULGUR, ASPARAGUS,
SNOW PEAS, BROCCOLI

•

SPA CARROT CAKE WITH
NORWICH SPA
WHIPPED CREAM

•

MIXED SEAFOOD GRILL

4 5 4
CALORIES PER SERVING

The secret to bringing off this dramatic-looking dish is preparing all the ingredients beforehand, because once cooking begins things move along pretty quickly. At the Spa we use a restaurant grill for the scallops and swordfish, but for the home cook, broiling is a more practical method.

1 cup raw bulgur
2 cups water
1 bunch broccoli
12 asparagus spears
16 snow pea pods
12 large sea scallops
6 ounces swordfish steak
4 1½-ounce fillets of sole
¾ to 1 cup dry white wine
½ recipe Tomato Ginger Coulis

Preheat the broiler.

Place the bulgur in a medium saucepan, add the water, and bring to a boil over high heat. Reduce the heat, cover, and simmer until the bulgur is tender, about 15 minutes. Fluff with a fork and keep warm in the top of a double boiler.

While the bulgur cooks, cut the broccoli into florets, reserving the stems for snacks or salads. Trim off the bottoms of the asparagus and peel the stems, if you wish. Break off the stem ends of the snow peas and pull off the strings.

Rinse and dry the scallops, trimming off any fibrous membrane. Cut the swordfish into 4 portions. Fold each sole fillet, envelope fashion, and place in a shallow baking dish. Sprinkle the fillets with the wine and cover the dish with a piece of parchment or foil.

Pour the coulis into a medium saucepan and place over moderate heat. When the sauce is almost at a boil, reduce the heat to very low, cover the saucepan, and keep the sauce hot while you cook the seafood and vegetables.

While the broiler heats, put the dish of sole fillets in the oven and bake the fish for about 5 to 7 minutes; do not overcook. Three minutes before the fillets are cooked, broil the scallops and swordfish for 1½ minutes on each side.

Meanwhile, bring 1 or 2 inches of water to a boil in the bottom of a steamer. Place the broccoli and asparagus in the steamer top and steam for 4 minutes. Add the snow peas and cook another 30 seconds. Remove the vegetables from the steamer and keep warm if the seafood has not yet finished cooking.

Ladle the coulis onto heated dinner plates and spread over the bottom with the back of the ladle. Spoon the bulgur into the center of the plates and arrange the seafood and vegetables around it. Serve at once.

Serves 4

TOMATO GINGER COULIS

2 5
CALORIES PER SERVING

This is a smooth tomato sauce with a nice bite of fresh ginger. Make it a day or two ahead of time and reheat just before using. Good with Boston Baked Halibut (page 62).

3 tablespoons peeled and grated fresh ginger
2 cups chopped onion
6 cups low-sodium canned peeled tomatoes, drained
¼ cup fresh lemon juice

Combine the ginger, onion, tomatoes, and lemon juice in a nonreactive saucepan, place over moderate heat, and bring to a boil. Cover the pan, reduce the heat, and simmer for 25 to 30 minutes, or until slightly reduced.

Transfer the sauce to a food processor, blender, or a small mill fitted with the fine blade, and puree. Strain through a fine sieve if pureed in a food processor. Let cool and store in a tightly covered container in the refrigerator.

Serves 8

SPA CARROT CAKE

128
CALORIES PER SERVING

We think this cake is one of our triumphs. It's moist and light, but substantial enough for you to know you're really eating dessert. We serve it here with Spa Whipped Cream, which adds 43 calories; the cake itself is 85 calories per serving. This makes 12 servings, so you'll have extra for the kids' after-school snacks or lunch boxes.

¾ cup grated carrots
½ cup unsweetened pineapple juice
⅔ cup whole wheat pastry flour
2 tablespoons cornstarch
1 teaspoon baking powder
½ teaspoon freshly grated nutmeg
½ teaspoon ground cinnamon
3 egg yolks, at room temperature
¼ cup honey
1 teaspoon vanilla extract
5 egg whites, at room temperature
½ teaspoon fresh lemon juice
½ recipe Norwich Spa Whipped Cream

Put the carrots and pineapple juice in a small glass or enamel saucepan and bring to a boil over moderate heat. Reduce the heat and simmer the carrots, uncovered, until they are tender but not mushy, about 5 to 7 minutes. Drain and let cool.

Preheat the oven to 325° F. Spray a 9-inch tube pan with vegetable cooking spray.

Sift the flour, cornstarch, baking powder, nutmeg, and cinnamon together onto a piece of wax paper. In a large mixing bowl, beat the egg yolks, honey, and vanilla until fluffy and lemon-colored. In another large bowl, whip the egg whites and lemon juice until stiff but not dry.

Fold the dry ingredients into the egg yolk mixture. Distribute the carrots over the top of the batter and fold in. Stir one-quarter of the egg whites into the batter to lighten it, then fold in the rest of the whites.

Turn the batter into the tube pan and bake in the center of the oven for 20 to 30 minutes, or until a toothpick inserted in the center of the cake comes out clean.

Place the cake, still in the pan, on a rack and leave for 10 minutes, then unmold the cake onto the rack and let it cool completely. Serve with whipped cream.

Serves 12

NORWICH SPA WHIPPED CREAM

43
CALORIES PER SERVING

This cream has two great advantages over whipped cream: it's very low in cholesterol and it keeps in the refrigerator for up to 2 days, holding its peaks quite nicely.

¼ cup skim milk
½ teaspoon unflavored gelatin
¼ cup cold water
⅔ cup nonfat dry milk
2 teaspoons fructose
1 teaspoon vanilla extract

Pour the milk into a metal mixing bowl and place in the freezer, along with the beaters. Let stand until the milk becomes slushy, 30 to 45 minutes.

In a small saucepan, sprinkle the gelatin over the cold water and let stand 2 or 3 minutes, or until the gelatin is softened. Place over very low heat and cook until the gelatin is dissolved.

Remove the skim milk and beaters from the freezer. Add the gelatin, dry milk, fructose, and vanilla and beat at high speed until soft peaks form. Cover the bowl and chill at least 15 to 20 minutes before serving.

Serves 8

DAY

3

U.S.A. NAVY
BEAN SOUP

245
CALORIES PER SERVING

Rich in protein and vitamins A and C, this hearty soup is the essence of New Spa Food—home cooking the way it really should be. The soup is easy to make, so double the recipe and freeze it in individual servings.

- 8 ounces dried navy beans
- 1 teaspoon extra-virgin olive oil
- 1½ teaspoons minced garlic
- ½ cup chopped onion
- 6 tablespoons chopped carrot
- 6 tablespoons chopped celery
- 1 small bay leaf
- 1 quart High-Potassium Vegetable Stock (page 143)
- 3 tablespoons plus 1 teaspoon chopped fresh herbs (chives, thyme, and basil are good choices)
- **Vegetable seasoning**
- **Freshly ground white pepper**

Pick over the beans, place them in a strainer, and rinse under cold running water. Soak the beans overnight in cold water to cover, changing the soaking water several times if you think of it. The next day, drain the beans and rinse them again.

In a heavy kettle, heat the oil over moderate heat. Add the garlic and onion and cook for 3 minutes, stirring often; do not allow the vegetables to brown. Stir in the carrot, celery, and bay leaf, cover the kettle, and reduce the heat a bit. Cook the vegetables for 10 minutes. Add the beans, stock, and 2 tablespoons of the fresh herbs and bring to a boil over high heat. Reduce the heat, partially cover, and cook the soup until the beans are tender, about 2 hours. Add vegetable seasoning and white pepper to taste.

Serve in heated soup bowls, each sprinkled with 1 teaspoon of herbs.

Serves 4

LEBANESE
CHOPPED SALAD

115
CALORIES PER SERVING

Summaht is a pungent Middle Eastern herb that is often used in place of lemon juice in marinades. It gives this salad a distinctive, elusive flavor. If you cannot find *summaht,* substitute any herb you like, especially oregano.

- 2 medium cucumbers
- 2 medium tomatoes
- ½ teaspoon chopped garlic
- 2 tablespoons chopped Italian parsley
- ¼ cup fresh lemon juice
- 2 tablespoons extra-virgin olive oil
- 1 teaspoon *summaht* (available at Middle Eastern food stores)
- ½ whole wheat pita bread
- 1 small head Boston lettuce
- 4 radicchio leaves

Peel the cucumbers, halve them lengthwise, and scrape out the seeds. Cut the cucumbers into ¼-inch slices and place in a mixing bowl. Remove the stem end from the tomatoes, cut them into ½-inch dice, and add to the cucumbers. Add the garlic, parsley, lemon juice, oil, and *summaht* and mix well. Cover the bowl and let the salad stand at least 1 hour in the refrigerator.

Meanwhile, preheat the oven to 250° F. Split the pita, cut it into small triangles, and place on a baking sheet. Toast the croutons for about 20 minutes, or until they are crisp.

Wash the Boston lettuce and spin dry. Arrange the lettuce and radicchio on salad plates, spoon in the cucumber mixture, and sprinkle with the pita croutons.

Serves 4

FALL FRUIT
COMPOTE

85
CALORIES PER SERVING

Here is a pretty dessert that can be prepared in less than 20 minutes. Use other firm ripe fruits, such as Italian plums or blanched, skinned peaches, or, in a pinch, add orange sections to the cooked fruit. The compote will keep for a day or two in the refrigerator.

- 2 cups apple juice
- 1 2-inch-strip orange zest (optional)
- 2 to 4 teaspoons fructose
- 1 medium pear (preferably Bosc or another variety that will hold its shape well)
- 1 medium Golden Delicious or Granny Smith apple
- 1 cup fresh or frozen cranberries
- Shredded orange zest

Pour the apple juice into a medium saucepan and add the strip of orange zest and the fructose. Bring to a boil over moderate heat.

Meanwhile, cut the pear into quarters and remove the core. Quarter the apple, cut out the core, and cut each quarter into 3 wedges. Rinse the cranberries and pick them over.

Add the pear, apple, and cranberries to the apple juice. Return it to a boil, then reduce the heat and simmer 5 to 7 minutes, or until the cranberries have popped and the apple and pear are cooked but not mushy.

Let the compote cool to room temperature. Transfer it to a bowl, cover, and refrigerate. To serve, divide the fruit among 4 plates, spoon some of the syrup over them, and garnish with shredded orange zest.

Serves 4

DINNER

578
CALORIES

•

ENDIVE AND BELL PEPPER SALAD
WITH NEW ENGLAND
"RANCH" DRESSING

•

SPINACH-STUFFED TURKEY BIRDS

•

WILD MUSHROOM SAUCE

•

RED BLISS POTATOES

•

STEAMED GREEN BEANS

•

CRANBERRY-ORANGE SHRUB

DAY

3

ENDIVE AND BELL PEPPER SALAD WITH NEW ENGLAND "RANCH" DRESSING

3 5
CALORIES PER SERVING

Our pleasantly tart buttermilk dressing tastes good on most greens and has far less fat and calories than conventional ranch dressings. Vary the flavor by adding ½ teaspoon of curry powder or ground cumin and a drop of hot pepper sauce.

4 medium heads Belgian endive
2 medium red bell peppers

NEW ENGLAND "RANCH" DRESSING
⅓ cup buttermilk
2 tablespoons plus 1 teaspoon low-fat plain yogurt
Fresh lemon juice
2 teaspoons chopped fresh dill
2 teaspoons chopped Italian parsley
½ teaspoon grated onion
Freshly ground white pepper

4 dill sprigs

Cut the stem end off the endive, then cut the heads lengthwise into julienne. Stem the peppers and cut out the seeds and white veins. Cut the peppers into thin julienne. Put the endive and peppers in a mixing bowl.

To make the dressing, in a small mixing bowl, whisk together the buttermilk, yogurt, a few drops of lemon juice, the dill, parsley, and onion. Add white pepper to taste and more lemon juice if needed. Pour the dressing over the endive and peppers, and toss to coat the vegetables lightly. Divide among 4 salad plates, top with a dill sprig, and serve.

Serves 4

SPINACH-STUFFED TURKEY BIRDS

3 7 3
CALORIES PER SERVING

This is a dish you might want to prepare in several stages, as described in the recipe. Boneless fresh turkey breast slices are inexpensive and low in calories, but a thin veal cutlet is a delectable alternative, though it will add close to 85 calories per serving.

4 turkey cutlets (cut from the leg, about 5 ounces each)
1 small onion, chopped
1 garlic clove, minced
½ cup dry white wine
12 ounces spinach, well washed and tough stems removed
1 tablespoon chopped Italian parsley
1 teaspoon chopped fresh thyme
2 teaspoons chopped fresh basil
1 teaspoon chopped fresh sage
Grated zest and juice of ½ lemon
½ cup Herbed Whole Wheat Bread Crumbs (page 140)
1 large egg, lightly beaten
1 cup Low-Sodium Chicken Stock (page 141)
1 cup Wild Mushroom Sauce
4 medium Red Bliss potatoes
Steamed Green Beans

Ask your butcher to trim the cutlets of any skin and membrane and then flatten them into scallops about ⅛ to ¼ inch thick. Or flatten them yourself between 2 sheets of wax paper. Chill the cutlets until ready to stuff them.

Preheat the oven to 350° F.

Spray a skillet with vegetable cooking spray, add the onion and garlic, and sauté over moderate heat until the onion is translucent, about 3 to 4 minutes. Add the wine, raise the heat, and add the spinach. Cook the spinach for about 2 minutes, or just until wilted, then transfer the mixture to a colander and let drain until the spinach is cool enough to handle. Gently squeeze

excess moisture from the spinach, place it in a bowl, and flavor it with the parsley, thyme, basil, and sage. Add the lemon zest and juice, bread crumbs, and egg; mix well.

Place the turkey cutlets on a work surface and spread them evenly with the spinach mixture. Roll up the cutlets, tucking in the sides, and seal with toothpicks.

(The recipe can be made ahead to this point. Place the turkey birds on a plate, cover with plastic wrap, and refrigerate until an hour before serving. Preheat the oven to 350° F. before proceeding.)

Spray a heavy skillet with vegetable cooking spray and place over moderate heat. Add the turkey birds and brown them on all sides, 5 to 7 minutes in all. Meanwhile, heat the stock to a simmer.

Transfer the turkey birds to a casserole just large enough to hold them, pour in the stock, and cover the casserole. Bake about 20 minutes. Remove the casserole from the oven and lower the oven to 200° F.

Drain off the juices from the veal (reserve for the sauce), cover the casserole again, and keep the turkey hot in the oven.

While the sauce is cooking, scrub the potatoes, place them in a medium saucepan, and add cold water to cover. Bring to a boil over high heat and boil the potatoes until tender, about 20 to 25 minutes. Drain and keep warm.

To serve, transfer the turkey birds to heated dinner plates and spoon the sauce over them. Add the potatoes and green beans to the plates and serve at once.

Serves 4

WILD MUSHROOM SAUCE

30
CALORIES PER SERVING

No pantry should be without a supply of dried mushrooms. Even in very small quantities, they supply so much flavor that once you've started cooking with them you'll find uses for them in a wide range of savory dishes. Cepes and morels are two of the more expensive dried (or fresh) mushrooms. In this recipe, dried Italian porcini (boletus), oyster mushrooms, shiitakes, or Polish boletus mushrooms can be substituted.

**Cooking liquid from turkey birds
plus enough Low Sodium Chicken
Stock (page 141) to make 1½ cups**
½ **ounce dried cepes**
½ **ounce dried morels**
1 **teaspoon low-sodium soy sauce**
½ **teaspoon fructose**
1 **tablespoon arrowroot dissolved in**
⅓ **cup cold water**

In a small saucepan combine the liquid, cepes, morels, soy sauce, and fructose and bring to a boil over high heat. Reduce the heat, cover the pan, and simmer gently for 20 minutes. The purpose here is to soften the mushrooms and flavor the broth, not to reduce the liquid.

Strain the broth into another saucepan. Chop the mushrooms, add them to the broth, and return the broth to the heat. Stir in the arrowroot mixture and cook just until the sauce is thickened, about 1 minute.

Makes 1½ cups

STEAMED GREEN BEANS

30
CALORIES PER SERVING

Steaming is one of the best ways to cook vegetables without salt or fat, and with no possibility of vitamins and minerals leaching out in boiling liquid. To test steamed green beans for doneness, dip your fingers in cold water and tweak a bean. If it bends a little, the beans are crisp-tender; if it bends a lot, the beans are fully cooked. The less you cook the beans, the more vitamins they retain.

1 **pound green beans**
Freshly grated nutmeg
Fresh lemon juice
Freshly cracked black peppercorns
2 **or 3 mushrooms (optional)**

Remove the ends from the beans and, if they are young and tender, leave them whole. Otherwise, cut the beans in half on the diagonal.

Bring water to a boil in the bottom of a steamer, put the beans in the top, and steam, covered, until the beans are cooked to your taste—about 5 minutes for tender but still quite crisp, up to 8 minutes for fully cooked.

Transfer the beans to a bowl and quickly toss them with a grating or two of nutmeg, a few drops of lemon juice, and cracked peppercorns to taste. Arrange the beans on the serving plates.

Slice the mushrooms and arrange a few slices over the beans.

Serves 4

CRANBERRY-ORANGE SHRUB

170
CALORIES PER SERVING

This rich pink dessert is similar to sorbet but lighter in texture.

1 **cup water plus 2 tablespoons
    cold water**
2 **cups cranberries**
½ **envelope unflavored gelatin**
¼ **cup honey**
1 **cup fresh orange juice**
2 **cups skim milk**
1 **egg white, at room temperature**

In a medium saucepan, bring 1 cup of water to a boil, add the cranberries, and reduce the heat. Simmer the fruit until it is soft, about 10 minutes. Put the cranberries through a food mill to remove the skins, or press through a sieve; keep warm.

Meanwhile, put the remaining 2 tablespoons of cold water in a large bowl, sprinkle the gelatin over it, and let the gelatin soften for 3 to 5 minutes. Stir in the hot cranberries and the honey and mix well to melt the gelatin and distribute it evenly throughout the fruit. Let cool to room temperature and stir in the orange juice. Cover the bowl and refrigerate until well chilled.

Beat in the milk, pour the mixture into a shallow metal dish, and freeze it until solid. Break it into chunks, transfer them to the bowl of a food processor fitted with the steel blade, and process until smooth. Alternatively, puree the mixture with a hand-held mixer.

Beat the egg white until it is stiff, fold it into the slush, and return the mixture to the freezing pan. Freeze the dessert for at least 30 minutes more. If it has frozen solid, transfer it to the refrigerator to soften for about 15 minutes. Serve in chilled goblets.

Serves 4

D A Y *4*

BREAKFAST

255
CALORIES
•
GRAPEFRUIT SECTIONS WITH
RASPBERRY PUREE
•
DELICIOUS OAT BRAN MUFFINS
•
DECAFFEINATED COFFEE OR TEA
•

LUNCH

373
CALORIES
•
MUSSELS FLORENTINE
•
CONNECTICUT BAKED APPLES
•
SPARKLING MINERAL WATER
•

GRAPEFRUIT SECTIONS WITH RASPBERRY PUREE

85
CALORIES PER SERVING

Our elegantly presented pinwheel of grapefruit sections in a pool of raspberry puree is an inviting start to your day. If separating the sections from their membranes is more than you care to face in the morning, simply drizzle the puree over cut grapefruit halves. Be sure the ingredients are cold before preparation begins.

2 medium pink grapefruit
2 cups raspberries or 1 10-ounce package frozen raspberries

As you peel the grapefruit, hold them over a bowl to catch the juice. With a sharp knife, cut away all the peel, pith, and outer membrane. Cut down to the core on either side of the inner membranes to free the segments, removing the pits with the point of the knife. Set the segments aside.

Squeeze the rinds and membrane over the bowl of juice and pour the juice into a food processor fitted with the steel blade. Add the raspberries to the processor and puree them.

Divide the puree evenly among 4 shallow soup bowls and arrange the grapefruit segments in a pinwheel design over the puree.

Serves 4

DELICIOUS OAT BRAN MUFFINS

170
CALORIES PER MUFFIN

The batter for these light, flavorful muffins must be prepared at least 9 hours in advance, ideally the night before you bake them. After that, the batter can be stored for up to 3 weeks in the refrigerator, which means you can treat yourself to fresh, individually baked muffins every morning. At the Spa we use oat bran cereal from a health food store, the kind served on Day 1 of our Spa program.

1¼ cups raw oat bran cereal
½ cup raisins
½ cup boiling water
2 tablespoons packed dark brown sugar
¼ cup light molasses
¼ cup blackstrap molasses
¼ cup safflower oil
1 large egg, beaten well
1 cup buttermilk
1¼ cups whole wheat flour
1¼ teaspoons baking soda
¼ teaspoon salt

At least 9 hours before serving, put half the oat bran cereal (½ cup plus 2 tablespoons) in a bowl, add the raisins, and stir in the boiling water. Set aside to cool.

In another mixing bowl, combine the remaining cereal with the brown sugar, molasses, oil, egg, and buttermilk and mix well. Sift together the flour, baking soda, and salt and stir into the buttermilk mixture. Stir in the cooled bran-raisin mixture. Cover the bowl tightly with plastic wrap and refrigerate for at least 8 hours.

Preheat the oven to 375° F. Line a muffin pan or as many individual custard cups as you wish with paper cupcake liners, or spray the pan or custard cups with vegetable cooking spray.

Stir the batter well (it will be quite thick) and, using an ice-cream scoop or a large spoon, half-fill the cups. Bake in the middle of the oven for 20 minutes. Do not overbake, or the muffins will dry out. Place the muffin pan or custard cups on a rack and allow the muffins to cool.

Store leftover batter, tightly covered with plastic wrap, in the refrigerator for up to 3 weeks, stirring it well just before using.

Makes 12 muffins

MUSSELS FLORENTINE

275
CALORIES PER SERVING

The rapid growth of the aquaculture industry has been a boon to seafood lovers. Shrimp, catfish, oysters, mussels, and salmon, among others, are now grown and harvested under controlled scientific conditions, making them widely available and much safer to eat. Cultivated mussels are not covered with sand and barnacles; they need only be rinsed and debearded, but well-cleaned ocean-grown mussels work just as well.

  6 ounces whole wheat or
    buckwheat pasta
  32 to 40 mussels
  ⅓ cup dry white wine
  2 large garlic cloves, minced (about
    5 teaspoons)
  1 teaspoon olive oil
  2 tablespoons grated onion
  1 pound spinach, well washed and
    tough stems removed
  2 tablespoons mixed chopped fresh
    tarragon and dill
  1 small tomato, chopped (about ½ cup)
  4 tablespoons chopped fresh basil

Bring 3 quarts of water to a boil in a large saucepan. Add the pasta and cook until al dente (tender but still firm to the bite), about 10 to 12 minutes, depending on the pasta. Drain, rinse well, cover, and keep warm.

Rinse the mussels under cold running water. If they are ocean mussels, scrub them under running water and pull off their beards; if they are farmed mussels, simply pull off the beards.

Place the mussels in a large kettle and add the wine, garlic, and about ½ cup of water. Cover the kettle, bring to a boil over high heat, and steam the mussels until they open. Begin checking after the mussels have cooked for about 4 minutes; it should take no longer than 6 to 8 minutes for them to open. Remove the mussels from their shells and keep them warm, discarding any that have not opened. (Strain the mussel juice through a cheesecloth-lined sieve and reserve for another use; it freezes well.)

In the meantime, in a large saucepan, heat the oil over moderate heat, add the onion, and cook until golden. Stir in the spinach and mixed herbs and cook just until the spinach is wilted, about 3 minutes.

To serve, divide the pasta among 4 heated plates. Spoon 1 tablespoon of the chopped tomato over each serving and sprinkle 1 tablespoon of basil over that. Surround the pasta with the spinach and arrange the mussels over the spinach. Serve immediately.

Serves 4

CONNECTICUT BAKED APPLES

98
CALORIES PER SERVING

A simple, homey dessert, these baked apples are discreetly flavored with cinnamon and maple sugar. You can add a dollop of nonfat yogurt sweetened with a little maple syrup to dress them up.

  4 medium red baking apples
    About ¼ cup unsweetened
    apple juice
  1 teaspoon ground cinnamon
  1 teaspoon maple sugar granules
    (available in health-food stores)
  ½ cup raspberries (optional)

Preheat the oven to 325° F.

Stem the apples, then core them without cutting through to the bottom. Remove a strip of peel around the stem end. Place the apples in a shallow baking dish just large enough to hold them. Pour enough apple juice into the hollowed-out cores to reach the top of the apples. Sprinkle cinnamon and maple sugar granules lightly over the apples and bake the fruit until it is slightly soft but not mushy, about 15 to 20 minutes.

Let the apples cool to room temperature and serve decorated with raspberries, if desired.

Serves 4

D A Y
4

D I N N E R

570
CALORIES

•

STONINGTON OR BLUSHING WINE SPRITZER

•

BIBB LETTUCE AND SNOW PEA SALAD
WITH LEMON VINAIGRETTE

•

SCALLOPED WINTER VEGETABLES

•

AMBROSIA SORBET

•

STONINGTON WINE SPRITZER

70
CALORIES PER SERVING

Some of our spa guests prefer to start their meals with a wine spritzer and pass on dessert, since spritzers are a refreshing way to enjoy wine while minimizing both calories and alcohol. The recipes that follow were given to us by Stonington Vineyards, a local Connecticut winery.

1 cup Seaport White or other dry
** white wine**
½ cup cranberry juice
8 ice cubes, crushed
1 cup sparkling mineral water
4 thin slices of orange, optional

Combine the white wine and cranberry juice together in a pitcher. Fill 4 goblets with crushed ice and divide the wine mixture among them. Fill with mineral water, and garnish with orange slices, if desired.

Serves 4

BLUSHING WINE SPRITZER

70
CALORIES PER SERVING

1 cup Seaport Blush or other
** blush wine**
2 cups sliced strawberries
8 ice cubes, crushed
4 thin slices lemon, optional

Process wine and strawberries in a blender. Fill 4 goblets with crushed ice, and divide the wine mixture among them. Garnish with lemon, if desired.

Serves 4

BIBB LETTUCE AND SNOW PEA SALAD WITH LEMON VINAIGRETTE

75
CALORIES PER SERVING

Bibb lettuce grows in small, compact heads. It's similar to the less pricey Boston lettuce—which can be used as a substitute—but is darker green with a slightly stronger flavor. Wash the leaves very carefully in three or four changes of water, because sand clings to them quite tenaciously. Eat one of the leaves before spinning them dry to be sure that they are completely free of sand.

4 heads bibb lettuce
32 snow pea pods, ends trimmed and
** strings pulled off**
1 lemon

LEMON VINAIGRETTE
2 teaspoons Dijon mustard
2 teaspoons extra-virgin olive oil
1 tablespoon fresh lemon juice,
** or to taste**
2 teaspoons snipped fresh chives or
** finely sliced scallion greens**
Fresh lemon thyme leaves or
** snipped fresh dill (optional)**
Freshly ground black pepper
2 to 3 teaspoons cold water

Arrange the lettuce on 4 salad plates.

Put the snow peas in a sieve and blanch them in boiling water for 30 seconds. Immediately plunge the sieve into a bowl of cold water to stop the cooking and set the color. Arrange the snow peas over the lettuce.

Using a citrus zester, cut strips from the lemon and strew them over the salad.

To make the vinaigrette, place the mustard and oil in a small bowl and whisk until emulsified. Stir in the lemon juice, herbs, and black pepper. Thin the dressing with cold water, adding 1 teaspoon at a time until it is the consistency of light cream. If you are making the vinaigrette ahead of time, cover and refrigerate, then whisk again just before drizzling it over the salad.

Serves 4

HAZELNUT OIL DRESSING

38
CALORIES PER SERVING

A somewhat earthier dressing than the lemon vinaigrette, this hazelnut oil blend is a delicious substitute. Costly hazelnut oil carries a high caloric tariff too, but a little adds a lot of delicate nut flavor. Be sure to keep the oil in the refrigerator; it goes rancid very quickly.

2 teaspoons hazelnut oil
1 teaspoon soy oil
2 teaspoons sherry vinegar
1 to 1½ tablespoons sparkling
** mineral water**
1½ tablespoons minced shallots
Freshly ground black pepper

In a small bowl, combine the oils, vinegar, mineral water, shallots, and a generous grinding of pepper. Cover the bowl and let the flavors mellow for 2 to 3 hours.

Serves 4

SCALLOPED WINTER VEGETABLES

3 6 0
CALORIES PER SERVING

Although the vegetables and cheese in this dish provide more than one-third the recommended daily allowance for protein, you may be someone who believes that the only real protein is meat. If that's the case, 3 to 4 ounces per serving of boneless, skinless chicken or turkey breast (about 1 pound in all), trimmed of all fat and cut into 1-inch chunks, can be added to the potatoes during the last 10 minutes of cooking. Chicken will add about 125 calories per serving and turkey breast only 100 to 110 calories. This recipe can be prepared in advance up to the final reheating.

2 medium celery root bulbs
2 tablespoons white wine vinegar
2 medium potatoes
2 turnips
2 carrots
3 large garlic cloves
2 large leeks (white part only)
2 or 3 parsnips
1 fennel bulb
½ onion
1 bay leaf
6 whole cloves
3 cups High-Potassium Vegetable Stock (page 143) or Low-Sodium Chicken Stock (page 141)
1 tablespoon chopped fresh sage or 1 pinch dried
1 tablespoon fresh thyme
1 tablespoon chopped fresh parsley Freshly ground white pepper (optional)
1 cup Herbed Whole Wheat Bread Crumbs (page 140)
½ cup freshly grated Asiago cheese

Trim the root end from the celery root and cut the bulbs into 1-inch pieces. Put the celery root in a medium bowl and add cold water to cover by 1 inch and the vinegar. Wash, peel, and quarter the potatoes and add to the bowl with the celery.

Trim the ends from the turnips and carrots, peel, and cut into 1-inch pieces. Set aside in a bowl. Mince the garlic and measure; you should have about 2 tablespoons. Add the garlic to the turnips and carrots.

Trim the root end from the leeks and wash them well. Cut into quarters lengthwise and then into 2-inch lengths. Set aside. Trim the end from the parsnips, peel, and cut into 1-inch lengths. Add to the leeks. Cut off the top, root, and outer leaves of the fennel, then cut into 1-inch pieces. Set aside with the leeks and parsnips. Cut a slit in the onion and insert the bay leaf; stud the onion with the cloves and add to the leek mixture.

Pour the stock into a large soup kettle and bring to a boil over high heat. Add the turnip mixture, reduce the heat to moderate, and cook, covered, at a slow boil for 10 minutes. Drain the celery root and potatoes and add to the pot, together with the leek mixture, sage, thyme, and parsley. Return to a boil and cook, covered, until the potatoes are tender, about 15 minutes.

Drain the vegetables, reserving the stock. Remove and reserve the potatoes, and place the remaining vegetables in a large shallow casserole.

Preheat the oven to 350° F.

Return the stock to the kettle and reduce it to 1½ cups over high heat. Meanwhile, mash the potatoes while they are still hot. Stir the potatoes into the stock and taste for seasoning, adding pepper to taste, if desired. Pour the sauce over the vegetables and sprinkle the top with the bread crumbs and cheese. Bake until the vegetables are heated through and the top is lightly browned, about 10 to 15 minutes. Serve at once.

Serves 4

AMBROSIA SORBET

6 5
CALORIES PER SERVING

A hand-turned ice-cream maker—many of them are reasonably priced and easy to use—is a worthwhile investment, giving you entrée to a myriad of wonderful, low-calorie sorbet recipes and even some for ice cream (see pages 47 and 145).

½ pineapple
1 cup fresh orange juice
1 teaspoon coconut extract (available in health-food stores)
¼ cup part-skim ricotta cheese
¼ cup unsweetened desiccated coconut

Cut the rind, eyes, and core from the pineapple. Cut the flesh into chunks and puree them in a food processor fitted with the steel blade. You should have about 2 cups of puree. Add the orange juice, coconut extract, and ricotta and process briefly.

Chill the mixture and freeze in an electric or hand-cranked ice-cream machine, following the manufacturer's instructions.

To make the sorbet in your freezer, transfer the mixture to a bowl and place in the freezer. When the liquid has frozen solid, about 2 to 3 hours, remove it from the freezer and, with a fork, break it into large chunks. Place the chunks in a food processor and process with the metal blade until smooth and creamy. Return to the bowl and freeze for at least 30 minutes more.

Preheat the oven to 350° F.

Spread the coconut on a baking sheet and toast in the oven for about 10 minutes, or until lightly colored, stirring 2 or 3 times. Alternatively, the coconut can be toasted in a toaster oven. Let cool.

To serve, place scoops of sorbet in dessert dishes and sprinkle with the toasted coconut.

Makes 1 quart, serving 6 to 8

D A Y

5

B R E A K F A S T

322
CALORIES

•

HOT APPLE PEAR DRINK OR
FRESH GRAPEFRUIT JUICE

•

PUMPKIN MUFFINS WITH
NUTMEG-FLAVORED YOGURT

•

DECAFFEINATED COFFEE OR TEA

•

LUNCH

433
CALORIES

•

AVGOLEMONO SOUP

•

SPAGHETTI SQUASH
PRIMAVERA

•

HONEYDEW MELON WITH LIME

•

HOT APPLE PEAR DRINK

65
CALORIES PER SERVING

While this doesn't have all the vitamin C of the fresh grapefruit juice we suggest with this breakfast, this fragrant, soothing toddy is packed with rich flavor, and with the muffin makes for a satisfying afternoon pick-me-up on a blustery fall day.

1 cup apple juice
1 cup pear nectar
1 cinnamon stick
3 apple cinnamon spice tea bags

Combine the fruit juices and cinnamon stick in a saucepan and bring to a simmer over low heat. Add the tea bags and simmer gently for approximately 20 minutes, until the flavors are blended.

Serves 4

FRESH GRAPEFRUIT JUICE

60
CALORIES PER SERVING

A refreshing change from orange juice, grapefruit juice is very high in vitamin C and potassium, and the pulp adds texture and fiber.

2 large Ruby red grapefruit

Chill the grapefruit overnight and squeeze them just before serving. Each grapefruit will yield 1 to 1⅓ cups of juice. Serve the juice in chilled glasses.

Serves 4

PUMPKIN MUFFINS WITH NUTMEG-FLAVORED YOGURT

240
CALORIES PER MUFFIN

Pumpkin is so much a part of New England's culinary history that this bright golden muffin was one of the first recipes created for the Norwich Spa. My daughter Samantha loves them for Halloween. The dry cereal, which gives the muffin some of its crunch, is another New England tradition. Like our bran muffins, these can be frozen. The yogurt adds 45 calories per serving.

2 cups whole wheat pastry flour
¾ cup nonfat dry milk
1 tablespoon baking powder
½ teaspoon ground allspice
½ teaspoon ground cinnamon
1 cup Grapenuts cereal
¾ cup raisins
2 large eggs
1 egg white
⅓ cup safflower oil
⅓ cup water
⅓ cup packed dark brown sugar
1⅓ cups unsweetened pumpkin puree
½ cup nonfat plain yogurt mixed with
¼ teaspoon freshly grated nutmeg, per serving (optional)

Preheat the oven to 350° F. Line a muffin pan with paper cupcake liners or use a nonstick pan.

Sift the flour, dry milk, baking powder, allspice, and cinnamon into a large mixing bowl. Stir in the Grapenuts and raisins. In another bowl, beat together the eggs, egg white, oil, water, sugar, and pumpkin puree. Add the egg mixture to the dry ingredients and stir just until combined.

Divide the batter among the muffin tins and bake the muffins for 15 to 20 minutes, or until golden brown. Place the muffin pan on a rack and let the muffins cool.

Serve with a dish of nutmeg-flavored yogurt, if desired.

Makes 12 muffins

AVGOLEMONO SOUP

175
CALORIES PER SERVING

A tongue twister to pronounce but delicious to taste, chewy brown rice adds another dimension to this Greek-inspired soup. All preparation can be done hours ahead of time; just reheat the soup and add the egg mixture right before serving.

6 cups Low-Sodium Chicken Stock (page 141)
½ cup raw brown rice
1 large egg
2 egg whites
¼ cup fresh lemon juice, or to taste
Vegetable seasoning
Freshly ground white pepper
Curly parsley sprigs
4 thin lemon slices

In a medium saucepan, bring the stock and rice to a boil over high heat. Reduce the heat, cover the pot, and cook the soup until the rice is tender, about 40 minutes. Meanwhile, put the egg, egg whites, and lemon juice in a medium bowl and whisk until well mixed.

Temper the egg mixture by slowly ladling in about ½ cup of the hot broth, stirring briskly as you do to prevent the eggs from cooking. Stir in another ½ cup of broth, then stir the egg mixture into the simmering soup. Cook just long enough to combine the eggs thoroughly with the soup, but do not allow the eggs to set. Turn off the heat and stir in the vegetable seasoning, pepper, and more lemon juice to taste.

Ladle the soup into heated bowls, sprinkle with the parsley, and float a lemon slice on top of each.

Serves 4

SPAGHETTI SQUASH PRIMAVERA

228
CALORIES PER SERVING

Pale yellow strands of spaghetti squash masquerade as the real thing in this light but satisfying lunch. The dish is most successful when the other vegetables are cooked briefly, so they retain their individual tastes and textures.

1 spaghetti squash (about 3 pounds)
1 cup broccoli florets
1 cup julienned green beans or 1-inch pieces asparagus spears
2 cups sliced mushrooms
1 large zucchini, cut into fine julienne
1 tablespoon extra-virgin olive oil
1½ teaspoons lemon pepper
6 tablespoons grated Asiago cheese
2 cups Light Tomato Sauce (page 140)

Preheat the oven to 350° F.

Pierce the spaghetti squash in several places with a fork, place it on a baking sheet, and bake for about 45 minutes, or until tender. (Alternatively, cut the squash in half lengthwise, scrape out the seeds, and bake, cut side down, for about 30 minutes.)

While the spaghetti squash bakes, steam the broccoli for 1 minute. Add the green beans and steam for 2 minutes more. Keep the vegetables warm, but do not allow them to cook any longer.

Spray a small skillet with vegetable cooking spray and place over moderately high heat. Add the mushrooms and sauté, tossing often, until they are lightly browned. Set aside.

When the spaghetti squash is cooked, lift it carefully and, with a fork, pull strands out of the shell into a bowl. Toss the squash with the zucchini, oil, and lemon pepper. Arrange the steamed broccoli and green beans over the squash and decorate with the mushrooms. Sprinkle with grated cheese and serve with a bowl of tomato sauce on the side.

Serves 4

HONEYDEW MELON WITH LIME

30
CALORIES PER SERVING

Cool green melon balls tickled with lime juice are a welcome palate cleanser. Some people like their melon chilled, but others insist that serving it at room temperature brings out the full flavor. Whichever serving method you prefer, be sure to choose a sweet, ripe melon by smelling, thumping, squeezing, or shaking it.

2 small honeydew melons
1 lime

Halve the melons and scrape out the seeds. Cut the flesh into 1-inch balls with a melon-baller and place them in a bowl.

With a zester, cut julienne strips from the lime. Squeeze the lime juice over the melon balls and toss to mix. Serve decorated with the lime zest.

Serves 4

D A Y
5

D I N N E R

480
CALORIES
•
ASPARAGUS FLAN
•
SALMON EN PAPILLOTE
•
POTATOES SPINACH
•
BLUEBERRY ICE CREAM
•
FLAVORED COFFEE
•

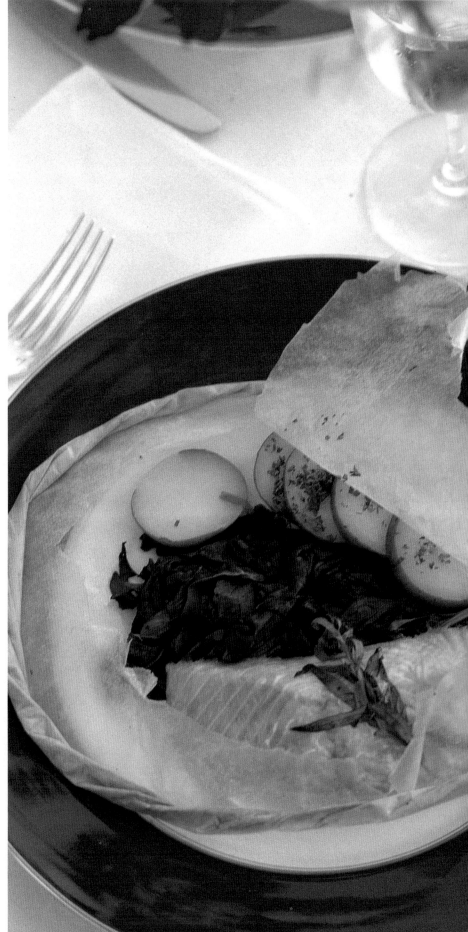

ASPARAGUS FLAN

91

CALORIES PER SERVING

Choose asparagus that is a rich green color, with a fresh appearance. The stalks should be firm but not woody, and the tips should be closed and compact.

1¼ pounds asparagus (about 36 pencil-thin spears or 15 to 18 medium to large spears)
1 teaspoon minced shallot
½ teaspoon minced garlic
⅓ cup low-fat plain yogurt
2 large eggs
1 egg white
Freshly grated nutmeg
Freshly ground white pepper

Wash the asparagus and trim the tough bottoms from the stalks. Cook the asparagus until it is just tender: 5 to 7 minutes in a large pot of boiling water or 4 to 5 minutes in a steamer. Drain the asparagus and plunge it into a bowl of cold water to stop the cooking. Drain again. Cut the tips off one-third of the spears 1½ inches from the top and reserve for decoration.

Preheat the oven to 325° F.

Cut the stalks and remaining asparagus into 1-inch pieces and place in a blender or food processor fitted with the steel blade. Add the shallot and garlic and process 2 to 3 minutes, or until the asparagus is pureed, stopping to scrape down the bowl once or twice.

Add the yogurt and continue processing. With the motor running, add the eggs and egg white and process 30 seconds more, or until they are incorporated. Strain the mixture through a medium sieve into a mixing bowl and season to taste with nutmeg and white pepper.

Spray four ½-cup custard cups or ramekins with vegetable cooking spray. Divide the asparagus mixture among the cups and place the cups in a shallow baking dish. Pour enough hot tap water into the dish to reach halfway up the custard cups. Cover the baking dish with foil. Bake the flans 40 to 45 minutes, or until they are set and a toothpick inserted in the center comes out clean. Be careful not to let the water in the baking dish boil, or the flans will curdle.

Run a thin-bladed knife around the outer edge of each custard and unmold on salad plates. Arrange the reserved asparagus tips around the flans to resemble the spokes of a wheel. Serve at once.

Serves 4

SALMON EN PAPILLOTE

280

CALORIES PER SERVING

At one time Connecticut's Thames River was the richest source of salmon in the United States. Sadly this is no longer true, and at the Inn we use mostly salmon flown in fresh from the West Coast.

Cooking in parchment is a time-honored method of preserving moisture, flavor, and texture. The paper can be bought in all kitchen-equipment stores and in the housewares sections of most department stores. Once you begin using it—to line baking pans, make paper cones for decorating, cut out stencil patterns, and so on—you'll find it indispensable. However, although foil makes a less dramatic presentation, it will do the job just as well.

4 medium Red Bliss potatoes
1 pound spinach, well washed and tough stems removed
1 tablespoon fresh tarragon leaves
¼ cup dry white wine
Vegetable seasoning
4 4-ounce skinless salmon fillets
4 tarragon sprigs

Wash the potatoes, place them in a saucepan with cold water to cover, and bring to a boil over high heat. Boil the potatoes until they are tender, about 20 minutes. Let cool and slice.

Put the spinach, tarragon, and wine in a large skillet and set over moderately high heat. Cook the spinach until it is wilted, letting most of the liquid evaporate without overcooking the spinach, 5 to 6 minutes. Add vegetable seasoning to taste and let the mixture cool.

Preheat the oven to 350° F. Fold 4 sheets of parchment or 12-inch squares of aluminum foil in half and cut into heart shapes. Open up the hearts and spray them on both sides with vegetable cooking spray.

To assemble the parchment packages, place the paper hearts on a flat surface. Divide the potatoes among the 4 hearts, placing them toward the top and to one side of the center fold. Put spinach and salmon on the same side of the fold as the potatoes. Top with a sprig of tarragon. Fold over the other side of the heart and crimp the edges, beginning at the top and making overlapping folds, taking care that the envelopes are securely fastened.

Place the packages on a baking sheet and bake 15 minutes, by which time the salmon will be cooked and the spinach and potatoes will be heated through.

Serves 4

BLUEBERRY ICE CREAM

105
CALORIES PER SERVING

Ricotta and cottage cheese provide a rich, creamy base for the intense flavor of blueberries. At only 105 calories per serving, this ice cream, made without questionable additives or artificial sweeteners, is miles ahead of any of the tofu or yogurt products that claim to be healthful.

> **8 ounces part-skim ricotta cheese**
> **8 ounces low-fat cottage cheese**
> **¼ cup fructose**
> **1 tablespoon vanilla extract**
> **2 cups fresh or unsweetened frozen blueberries**

In the bowl of a food processor fitted with the steel blade, combine the ricotta, cottage cheese, fructose, and vanilla and process until blended. Add the blueberries and process again until the blueberries are pureed.

Chill the mixture and freeze in an electric or hand-cranked ice-cream maker, following the manufacturer's instructions.

Serve in chilled goblets.

Makes 1 quart, serving 6 to 8

FLAVORED COFFEE

4
CALORIES PER SERVING

Serving a flavored coffee with—or in place of—dessert always seems to make a meal more special. Many different varieties are available at gourmet coffee shops or from mail-order sources, ranging from those with essences of liqueurs or fruits to rich-tasting chocolate and spice flavors. If you do decide to purchase flavored coffees, try combining two different flavors to make your own unique blend, one that complements the dessert you'll be serving it with. Or try creating your own flavored brews at home. Always start with freshly ground decaffeinated coffee beans and only grind as much as you need at a time. That way you get the most robust flavor from your beans.

Here are some suggestions to try: To 2½ to 3 ounces ground coffee beans add

- 1 whole vanilla bean that has been ground in a spice or coffee grinder;
- the grated rind of 1 whole orange, 1 whole lemon, and ¼ teaspoon ground cloves;
- 2½ to 3 tablespoons carob powder;
- 3 tablespoons dried mint.

Mix well, then brew as usual. Serve piping hot, or chill and serve over ice in tall glasses, garnished with a spring of mint or a slice of orange.

Serves 4

SPA

BANANA-BERRY TREAT

•

ORANGE COOLER

•

MINIATURE ZUCCHINI MUFFINS

•

GIARDINERA

•

WHOLE WHEAT PIZZAS

SNACKS

BANANA-BERRY TREAT

80
CALORIES PER SERVING

A luscious pick-me-up for after a workout, this drink is similar to our Strawberry Buttermilk Sherbet but much faster to make. Chilling all ingredients before you begin will make the drink froth higher.

1 banana
¾ cup berries (strawberries, huckleberries, blackberries)
1½ tablespoons honey
¼ cup buttermilk
½ cup ice cubes

Peel the banana, cut into chunks, and place in a blender or food processor fitted with the steel blade. Add the berries, honey, buttermilk, and ice cubes. Process until the fruit is pureed and the drink is frothy. Serve in chilled glasses.

Serves 4

ORANGE COOLER

70
CALORIES PER SERVING

Honey and vanilla perfume this creamy cooler. Be sure ingredients are chilled before you begin.

1 cup fresh orange juice
½ cup sliced banana
1 tablespoon honey
1 teaspoon vanilla extract
2 tablespoons nonfat plain yogurt
1 cup ice cubes

Place the orange juice, banana, honey, vanilla, yogurt, and ice cubes in a blender or food processor and process until pureed. Serve in chilled glasses.

Serves 4

MINIATURE ZUCCHINI MUFFINS

106
CALORIES PER MUFFIN

Serve these adorable morsels for tea, as we do on page 132, or at breakfast with fruit-only preserves and some yogurt, or simply enjoy them as a snack.

¼ cup packed dark brown sugar
2 tablespoons honey
1 large egg
3 egg whites
6 tablespoons safflower oil
1¼ cups grated zucchini
1½ cups whole wheat flour
½ teaspoon baking powder
1 teaspoon ground cinnamon
¼ cup chopped walnuts
¼ cup raisins, plumped for 20 minutes in ½ cup hot water and drained

Preheat the oven to 350° F. Spray 20 miniature muffin tins with vegetable cooking spray.

Put the sugar, honey, egg, and egg whites in a mixing bowl and beat with an electric mixer at moderately high speed until well blended. Add the oil and continue beating until the ingredients are well mixed and lemon-colored. Wrap the zucchini in a kitchen towel and twist to wring out the moisture. Stir the zucchini into the sugar mixture.

Sift together the flour, baking powder, and cinnamon. Gradually add the flour mixture to the zucchini mixture, then stir in the nuts and raisins. Drop the batter into the muffin tins and bake for about 25 minutes, or until the tops are golden.

Makes 20 miniature muffins

GIARDINERA

124
CALORIES PER SERVING

In this traditional Italian *salumeria* offering, a colorful array of vegetables is quickly blanched and then marinated in a spicy vinaigrette. Since vinegar is the dominant element in the marinade, use one that's mellow and winy, without any harsh overtones. Make giardinera in quantity—the recipe can be doubled or even tripled quite easily—and serve it on a buffet table.

2 medium carrots, peeled
1 small red bell pepper
1 small yellow bell pepper
2 cups broccoli florets
1 cup cauliflower florets
¼ cup pitted black olives, drained
½ cup pepperoncini, drained
1 tablespoon chopped Italian parsley

MARINADE
¼ cup extra-virgin olive oil
1 cup white wine vinegar
¼ cup mineral water
1 tablespoon Dijon mustard
Cracked black peppercorns
Vegetable seasoning

1½ tablespoons chopped fresh oregano

Cut the carrots into ¼-inch diagonal slices. Core the bell peppers, cut them into ¼-inch strips, and set aside.

Bring a saucepan of water to a boil and prepare a large bowl of ice water. In the saucepan, blanch the carrots for about 4 minutes, or until brightly colored but still very crunchy. With a slotted spoon, transfer the carrots to the ice water to stop the cooking and set the color. Add the broccoli to the blanching pan, cook it for about 2 minutes, then transfer to the ice water. Cook the cauliflower for 3 to 4 minutes, then put it in the ice water.

When the vegetables are cool, drain them and place in a mixing bowl. Add the bell peppers, olives, and pepperoncini and toss to mix. Add the parsley and toss again.

To make the marinade, combine the oil, vinegar, mineral water, mustard, and black pepper and vegetable seasoning to taste and whisk well.

Pour the marinade over the vegetables, cover, and refrigerate for 3 or 4 hours or overnight. (Do not prepare this recipe more than a day in advance. After long marination, the broccoli turns yellowish green and the flavor of the broccoli and cauliflower overwhelms those of the other ingredients.)

Drain the vegetables before serving and sprinkle with oregano.

Serves 4 to 6

WHOLE WHEAT PIZZA WITH LEMON-MINT TOPPING

1 4 5
CALORIES PER PIZZA

Who can resist festive spa pizzas, with their crisp, high-protein crusts and mouth-watering toppings? This heady Mediterranean version (and the variations that follow) makes 8 snack or appetizer servings, but it would also serve 4 as a wonderful main course for lunch or supper, preceded by a light soup and followed by salad and fruit.

6 garlic cloves or to taste
3 cups fresh mint leaves
Juice of 1 lemon
2 tablespoons extra-virgin olive oil
16 partially baked miniature Whole Wheat Pizza Crusts (page 144)
16 fresh mint leaves

Place the garlic, mint leaves, lemon juice, and oil in the bowl of a food processor fitted with the steel blade and process until the mixture forms a paste.

Place 2 tablespoons on each pizza crust and spread to within ¼ inch of the edge. Bake 8 to 10 minutes, or until the bottoms of the crusts are crisp. Place a whole mint leaf on each pizza and serve at once.

Serves 8

VARIATION: TOMATO, ARTICHOKE AND FRESH HERB TOPPING

1 4 8
CALORIES PER PIZZA

Arrange 2 or 3 thin slices of plum tomato on each pizza crust and top with 1 or 2 pieces of marinated artichoke hearts. Bake 3 to 5 minutes, sprinkle with a bit of grated Asiago cheese, and bake 5 minutes longer.

VARIATION: GRILLED VEGETABLE TOPPING

1 4 8
CALORIES PER PIZZA

Top each pizza with slices of eggplant, bell pepper, and red onion that have been grilled with a light brushing of olive oil and a sprinkle of oregano. Add slices of fresh tomato and more fresh oregano and bake 8 to 10 minutes.

VARIATION: WILD MUSHROOM AND ONION TOPPING

1 4 2
CALORIES PER PIZZA

Sauté onions and garlic in a little bit of olive oil, then add sliced fresh oyster and shiitake or other wild mushrooms. Season with fresh thyme leaves and spoon onto pizza crusts. Bake for 8 to 10 minutes.

In the years since I opened my first spa, Americans have become so knowledgeable about fitness, diet, and nutrition that they regard healthy eating as a form of enlightened self-interest. They know that diet is one of the few things we can do for ourselves that has an immediate impact on how we look and feel. A regular feature at the Norwich Inn and Spa is an after-dinner discussion group and demonstration, which might be called "Spa Cooking in Theory and Practice." It's one of the ways we show our guests how to bring our real-life Spa experience into their everyday lives.

That theory and practice can best be summed up in the term "Yankee Ingenuity" or the ability to make the best use of the means at hand. Yankee Ingenuity is the way I describe our resourceful approach to food, the inventive way we adapt ordinary food to meet Spa standards, and our imaginative use of common ingredients. It is the spirit that informs all of the New Spa Food programs, and it's also the name we've given to the 1,550-calorie-a-day menus created for men on weight-loss diets and for active women on maintenance regimens.

The dinner for Day 1 is a practical demonstration of Yankee Ingenuity. If we'd followed standard recipes for each dish in this delicious, homey meal, the total calories for dinner would come close to 1,670. Using Yankee Ingenuity, we transformed the dinner into New Spa Food at a total of 637 calories for the entire meal, with the virtual elimination of all cholesterol and, most important, without any sacrifice in flavor.

Here's how we did it: steamed clams, almost a cliché in New England, are usually accompanied by melted butter. Our cherrystones are cooked in a heady brew of white wine, diced tomatoes, jalapeño peppers, and chopped herbs, a broth so flavorful that there's no need for butter. Total calories, just 50 per serving.

In a conventional cookbook recipe for Boston-style halibut, the fish fillets would be dusted with flour, dipped in beaten egg, coated thickly with bread crumbs, and deep-fried. Delicious, it's true, and at least 500 calories a serving. We decided to season the bread crumbs with basil and thyme, dust them over baked halibut fillets, and toast them in the broiler. Also delicious, and only 170 calories a serving.

Potatoes boulanger is a gratin of thinly sliced potatoes and onions. Unlike escalloped potatoes, which would normally be baked in milk and heavy cream, for a calorie count of more than 500 per serving, ours substitutes rich homemade chicken stock and subtle seasonings, eliminating nearly all the cholesterol and 300 calories per serving.

Our recipe for carrots and peppers shows how Yankee Ingenuity can give new life to even the most prosaic ingredients. The carrots are quickly cooked, lightly coated with a spicy mixture of cumin, lemon juice, garlic, shallots, soy sauce, and stock, and then sprinkled with chopped coriander—all for just 70 calories per serving.

Finally, the clafouti, a classic dessert from the French Limousin, has been reinterpreted for the Spa menu; it now contains only one egg, instead of three, and uses evaporated skim milk rather than whole milk and cream. The smooth kirsch-scented custard bursting with fresh cherries is still delicious, but most of the cholesterol has been eliminated and the calories have been reduced by more than half, to just 144 per serving.

Most Yankee Ingenuity "methods" entail nothing more than applying good judgment to the foods you prepare:

• Use only the freshest, best fruits, vegetables, fish, and seafood. Many of these items are at their least expensive when they're in season (Yankees have been known to pinch a penny here and there), and that's when they taste best.

• Always use skim milk or evaporated skim milk instead of whole milk or heavy cream.

• Use egg whites instead of or to supplement whole eggs.

• Low-sodium homemade stocks, which average about 30 calories per cup, improve the taste of soups, stews, and sauces, and they can be boiled down to make intensely flavorful reductions.

• When you convert a conventional recipe to New Spa Food, begin by eliminating at least half the fat or oil. If butter is called for, substitute corn oil margarine; if oil is specified, try to use olive oil or a polyunsaturated oil. When possible, eliminate the fat altogether and use vegetable cooking spray for sautéeing, greasing baking tins, or sweating vegetables for soups and sauces.

• Nonfat yogurt actually tastes better than low-fat yogurt, so use it as a spread, for salad dressings, and as a topping for baked potatoes. Low-fat cottage cheese, whirled in a blender, makes a good cream cheese substitute.

• Save a lot of calories by substituting fructose for sugar. Although teaspoon for teaspoon they have the same number of calories, fructose has twice the sweetening power of sugar, so you'll use less of it. Pureed fruit also adds sweetness to many dishes, plus a healthy dose of vitamins and fiber.

These are the common sense precepts of Yankee Ingenuity, but New Spa Food is not created by common sense alone, or by rote substitution of one ingredient for another; use your imagination and experiment—you'll be amazed at how easy it becomes.

D A Y
1

B R E A K F A S T

3 4 0
CALORIES

•

CHERRY-GINSENG BREW

•

FRUIT TOAST WITH
FLAVORED POT CHEESE

•

L U N C H

6 3 5
CALORIES

•

BROCCOLI AND BASIL SOUP

•

SEVEN-GRAIN KASHI SALAD

•

SLICED MANGO WITH
MINTED MELON SAUCE

•

CHERRY-GINSENG BREW

75

CALORIES PER SERVING

A subtle hint of ginseng makes this flavorful brew just a bit exotic. You can substitute concord grape juice for the black cherry juice if it is easier to find.

2 cups black cherry juice or concord grape juice
2 cups water
3 lemon herbal teabags
1 ginseng teabag

Combine the juice, water, and teabags in a saucepan and simmer gently until the flavors marry, about 5 minutes.

Serves 4

FRUIT TOAST WITH FLAVORED POT CHEESE

265

CALORIES PER SERVING

This dazzling breakfast takes no time at all to prepare. All you need is 4 generous cups of several kinds of fruit and a few minutes to arrange them on toast. We add orange extract to the cheese for an intense fruit flavor, but you can use orange juice if you prefer, or even orange flower water, which will lend its own perfume.

1 cup sliced strawberries
2 kiwis, peeled and sliced
½ cup pitted and halved cherries
½ cup raspberries
1 large banana, peeled and sliced
4 slices whole-grain bread, toasted

ORANGE-FLAVORED POT CHEESE
1 cup pot cheese
1 teaspoon grated orange zest
¼ teaspoon orange extract
Fine orange zest julienne

Preheat the oven to 350° F.
Arrange the fruit decoratively in stripes on the toast. Place the toast on a baking sheet and bake for 5 to 10 minutes, or until the fruit is heated.
While the toast is baking, combine the pot cheese, grated zest, and orange extract in a bowl and mash until well blended.
Arrange the toast on heated plates and serve with the cheese, garnished with the orange zest and julienne.

Serves 4

BROCCOLI AND BASIL SOUP

120

CALORIES PER SERVING

This thick, garlicky soup has a creamy texture although it's made without cream or milk. Served hot or cold, it's fine picnic fare.

2 cups Low-Sodium Chicken Stock (page 141)
4 cups coarsely chopped broccoli (florets and stems)
1 cup coarsely chopped onions
1 tablespoon unsalted butter
1 tablespoon extra-virgin olive oil
3 garlic cloves
¼ cup chopped fresh basil
Vegetable seasoning
Fresh lemon juice
4 basil sprigs

In a medium saucepan, bring the stock to a simmer over moderate heat. Add the broccoli and onions, reduce the heat, and simmer, covered, until tender, 8 to 10 minutes.
Transfer the soup to the bowl of a food processor fitted with the steel blade and process until smooth. Reserve the soup in the processor bowl.
Put the butter and oil in the original saucepan, and place over moderate heat to melt the butter. Add the garlic and sauté until golden, 2 to 3 minutes. Scrape the garlic into the food processor bowl, add the basil, and process until smooth.
Chill the soup, if you wish to serve it cold, then add vegetable seasoning and lemon juice to taste. Serve garnished with the sprigs of basil.
To serve hot, return the soup to the saucepan, stir in the vegetable seasoning and lemon juice, and bring to a simmer *briefly* over moderate heat. Serve in heated soup bowls garnished with the basil sprigs.

Serves 4

SEVEN-GRAIN KASHI SALAD

390
CALORIES PER SERVING

Kashi, the Breakfast Pilaf, is a combination of seven whole grains—winter wheat, long-grain brown rice, oats, triticale, rye, raw buckwheat, and barley—and sesame seeds—which, when cooked, becomes a pilaf with a deliciously varied texture and nutty flavor. We make this colorful salad with a crunchy mixture of fresh raw vegetables: zucchini; yellow squash; carrots; red, green, and yellow bell peppers; scallions; tomatoes; celery; and mushrooms—whatever is best at the market. The salad can be made the night before, then packed in a tightly covered container until lunch—at home or away.

- 2 cups water
- 1 cup Kashi
- 2 cups mixed raw vegetables cut into ¼-inch dice
- ½ cup chopped fresh chervil or Italian parsley
- ¼ cup snipped fresh chives

DRESSING
- 2 tablespoons Dijon mustard
- ¼ cup safflower oil
- ¼ cup rice wine vinegar
- ¼ cup red wine vinegar
- ¼ cup light soy sauce
- 1 teaspoon grated fresh ginger
- Dash of freshly ground white pepper

- 1 small head green leaf or Boston lettuce
- 1 small head radicchio
- 2 red tomatoes
- 2 yellow tomatoes (optional)
- 4 scallion flowers (optional)
- Fresh chervil sprigs (optional)

Bring the water to a boil in a medium saucepan over high heat, add the Kashi, and reduce the heat to medium. Cook the Kashi, uncovered, at a slow boil for 25 minutes, or until the grains are tender and the water is absorbed. Check once or twice near the end of cooking and add about ¼ cup of water if necessary to keep the Kashi from sticking to the pan. Let cool to room temperature and chill.

Put the cooked Kashi, diced vegetables, chervil, and chives in a large mixing bowl and toss gently to combine.

To make the dressing, whisk together the mustard and oil in a small mixing bowl. Slowly whisk in the vinegars and soy sauce, then stir in the ginger and pepper. Pour three-quarters of the dressing over salad and toss lightly.

On a large platter or on individual plates, arrange the lettuce, radicchio, tomatoes, and Kashi salad. Decorate with scallion flowers and chervil sprigs, if desired, and drizzle on the remaining dressing.

SLICED MANGO WITH MINTED MELON SAUCE

125
CALORIES PER SERVING

Black pepper adds a spirited touch to this dish, or stir a teaspoon or two of green crème de menthe (less than 20 calories per teaspoon) into the melon sauce and omit the pepper. Use ripe mangoes, which give off a wonderful aroma and are somewhat soft to the touch but not mushy. Unless you are preparing the dessert ahead of time and can refrigerate it, all ingredients should be cold.

- 2 large mangoes, chilled
- ½ large honeydew melon, chilled
- ¼ to ½ cup chopped fresh mint
- Freshly ground black pepper
- 4 sprigs mint

Peel the mangoes with a vegetable peeler. With a sharp knife, mark the pulp into quarters, cutting down vertically to the pit. Carefully cut the pulp from the pit by scraping the knife down the flat sides of the pit from stem end to bottom. Cut the pulp into slices and arrange on dessert plates.

Place the honeydew and mint in the bowl of a food processor fitted with the steel blade and puree. Strain the puree through a very fine sieve, discarding the liquid. Spoon the puree onto the dessert plates and grind black pepper over it. Decorate with the mint sprigs.

D A Y

1

D I N N E R

5 1 5
CALORIES

•

MEXICALI STEAMED CLAMS

•

BOSTON BAKED HALIBUT

•

POTATOES BOULANGER

•

MEDITERRANEAN-SPICED CARROTS
AND PEPPERS

•

CHERRY CLAFOUTI OR
ORANGE GRAPENUT PUDDING

•

MEXICALI STEAMED CLAMS

50
CALORIES PER SERVING

Jalapeño peppers add a little fire to plump, juicy clams steamed with white wine and garlic. The juices and seeds of jalapeño are very hot, and the peppers should be handled with care. If possible, wear rubber gloves when working with chilies, wash all utensils thoroughly, and keep the juices away from your eyes.

20 cherrystone clams
1 medium tomato
2 jalapeño peppers
1½ tablespoons minced shallots
3 or 4 garlic cloves, minced
1 cup dry white wine
1 teaspoon chopped fresh coriander
1 tablespoon chopped fresh basil
1 teaspoon chopped Italian parsley

Scrub the clams well under running water to remove all the sand. Set aside. Cut the tomato in half crosswise and, cupping each half in your palm, gently squeeze out the juice and seeds. Cut the tomato into ¼-inch dice and reserve. Cut off and discard the stem ends of the jalapeño peppers, cut the peppers in half lengthwise, and scrape out and discard the seeds. Cut the peppers into fine julienne and reserve.

Heat a saucepan over moderate heat, spray with vegetable cooking spray, and add the shallots and garlic. Cook for 2 to 3 minutes, but do not allow to brown. Add the wine and jalapeño peppers and bring to a boil. Add the clams and tomato, cover the pan tightly, and steam the clams for 5 to 8 minutes, or until they are all open. Discard any clams that have not opened by this time.

Add the coriander, basil, and parsley and toss with the clams. Transfer the clams to heated wide soup plates and spoon some of the broth over each portion.

Serves 4

BOSTON BAKED HALIBUT

170
CALORIES PER SERVING

Perfectly fresh halibut tastes so good it needs scarcely any embellishment. Here, herb-scented bread crumbs are sprinkled over the fillets and browned under the broiler. Add half a teaspoon of grated lemon zest to the crumbs for a little variety.

4 4-ounce halibut fillets
1 cup whole wheat bread crumbs
** (made from 2 to 3 slices bread)**
1 teaspoon chopped Italian parsley
½ teaspoon chopped fresh basil
½ teaspoon chopped fresh thyme
** Vegetable seasoning**
** Freshly ground black or**
** white pepper**
** Chopped Italian parsley**
4 lemon wedges (optional)

Preheat the oven to 350° F. Spray a baking dish with vegetable cooking spray.

Arrange the halibut in the baking dish, cover with foil, and bake for about 8 minutes, or until the fish is almost cooked.

Meanwhile, in a shallow bowl combine the bread crumbs, parsley, basil, thyme, and vegetable seasoning and pepper to taste. Remove the baking dish from the oven and sprinkle the crumbs over the fillets. Return the fish to the oven and bake 2 to 3 minutes longer, or until the bread crumbs are browned and the fish flakes easily. Serve sprinkled with parsley on heated plates, with lemon wedges, if desired.

Serves 4

POTATOES BOULANGER

80
CALORIES PER SERVING

This is our Spa interpretation of a hearty French country gratin of potatoes and onion. A flavorful chicken stock is crucial to the success of this dish, which is made without the usual enhancements of butter and heavy cream.

2 medium russet potatoes
** (about 1 pound)**
1 large Spanish onion
1 garlic clove
** Freshly ground white pepper**
** Freshly grated nutmeg**
1 to 1½ cups Low-Sodium Chicken
** Stock (page 141), heated**

Preheat the oven to 350° F.

Wash and peel the potatoes. Slice them ¼ inch thick and place them in a saucepan with water to cover. Bring to a boil and cook just until parboiled, about 5 minutes. Drain and set aside.

Slice the onion. Heat a medium skillet over moderate heat, spray with vegetable cooking spray, and sauté the onion and garlic until they are translucent, about 5 minutes. Leave the onion mixture in the skillet.

Drain the potatoes and season them with pepper and nutmeg to taste. Add them to the skillet and mix well with the onion and garlic. Transfer the mixture to a 9 x 12-inch shallow oval casserole, pour in enough stock to reach the top of the potatoes, and bake for about 1½ hours, or until the potatoes are cooked and most of the stock has been absorbed. Check the potatoes several times toward the end of cooking and add more stock as needed. Serve at once.

Serves 4

MEDITERRANEAN-SPICED CARROTS AND PEPPERS

71
CALORIES PER SERVING

Carrots and red peppers are seasoned with a piquant combination of cumin, lemon juice, garlic, soy sauce, and fresh coriander.

4 or 5 large carrots, peeled
½ cup chopped red bell pepper
1 cup High-Potassium Vegetable Stock (page 143) or Low-Sodium Chicken Stock (page 141)
1 teaspoon ground cumin
1 tablespoon fresh lemon juice
1 tablespoon minced garlic
1 tablespoon chopped shallots
1 tablespoon low-sodium soy sauce
Vegetable seasoning
1½ teaspoons arrowroot mixed with 1½ teaspoons cold water
2 to 3 tablespoons chopped fresh coriander

Cut the carrots into ¼-inch diagonal slices and steam them until they are crisp-tender, about 5 minutes, adding the bell pepper after 4 minutes. Keep warm.

Meanwhile, in a saucepan over moderate heat, bring to a boil the stock, cumin, lemon juice, garlic, shallots, soy sauce, and vegetable seasoning to taste. Stir in the arrowroot mixture and simmer the sauce, stirring, until it is thickened and clear, 1 to 2 minutes. Add the carrots and peppers, stirring gently to coat with the sauce. Serve sprinkled with coriander.

Serves 4

CHERRY CLAFOUTI

144
CALORIES PER SERVING

Clafouti, another French country dish, is a custard baked with fresh fruit. Traditionally, sweet cherries are used, but the dessert is often made with Italian prune plums, halved, pitted, and cut into ½-inch pieces. If you do use plums, substitute mirabelle (plum brandy) for the kirschwasser.

1 cup Bing cherries
4 teaspoons kirschwasser or cherry brandy
2 tablespoons whole wheat flour
1½ tablespoons fructose
10 ounces (½ cup plus 2 tablespoons) evaporated skim milk
1 large egg, beaten
1 teaspoon vanilla extract
Confectioners' sugar or 1 or 2 pinches of fructose pulverized with a mortar and pestle (optional)

Preheat the oven to 325° F.

Spray four ½-cup ramekins with vegetable cooking spray and divide the cherries among them. Sprinkle 1 teaspoon kirsch over each ramekin.

In a medium bowl, combine the flour and fructose. Stir in the evaporated milk, egg, and vanilla and whisk until well blended. Divide the mixture evenly among the ramekins.

Place the ramekins in a baking dish and add enough hot tap water to reach halfway up their sides. Bake the clafoutis for 30 minutes, or until the perimeters are set but the centers are still soft. Serve warm, lightly dusted with confectioners' sugar, if desired.

Serves 4

ORANGE GRAPENUT PUDDING

125
CALORIES PER SERVING

This traditional New England favorite, shown in the photograph on page 101, is a wonderful alternative to the Clafouti, especially during the winter months when fresh cherries can be hard to come by.

1 large egg
1 egg white
½ cup fructose
2 cups skim milk
½ teaspoon vanilla extract
½ teaspoon orange extract
1½ teaspoons grated orange zest
2 tablespoons Grapenuts cereal
Freshly grated nutmeg

Preheat the oven to 300° F.

Put the egg, egg white, and fructose in a medium mixing bowl and whisk until well mixed. Add the milk slowly, then whisk in the vanilla and orange extracts and the orange zest.

Put 1½ teaspoons of Grapenuts in the bottom of each of five 4-ounce custard cups and pour the custard mixture over them. Sprinkle the custard with nutmeg.

Place the cups in a shallow baking dish, add enough very hot tap water to the pan to reach halfway up the cups, and bake the custards 20 to 25 minutes, or until set.

Remove the custards from the water bath and let cool. Refrigerate until ready to serve.

Serves 5

D A Y

2

B R E A K F A S T

3 3 2
CALORIES

•

FRESH SPICED
TOMATO DRINK

•

HERBED SPA OMELET

•

TOAST

•

DECAFFEINATED
COFFEE OR TEA

•

L U N C H

5 0 5
CALORIES

•

STEAMED VEGETABLES
WITH RED BASMATI RICE

•

PEPPER PEANUT
AND SWEET AND SOUR
DIPPING SAUCES

•

APRICOT MOUSSE

•

FRESH SPICED TOMATO DRINK

40
CALORIES PER SERVING

This thick, zesty drink is similar in texture to gazpacho and for a weekend brunch it makes the best Bloody Mary mixer you'll ever taste. The seasonings can be adjusted to your taste. Prepare the drink the night before and process with ice cubes just before serving.

- 6 ounces low-sodium tomato juice cocktail or tomato juice
- 6 ounces low-sodium canned tomatoes
- 1 celery stalk, strings scraped off and roughly chopped
- 1 small carrot, peeled and roughly chopped
- ½ medium cucumber, peeled, seeded, and roughly chopped
- ½ medium green bell pepper, seeded and roughly chopped
- 1 scallion (white part only), sliced
- 1 garlic clove, minced
- ¼ teaspoon hot pepper sauce
- ½ teaspoon Worcestershire sauce
  Juice of 1 lime
- 1 teaspoon rice wine vinegar
- 1 cup ice cubes

Place all ingredients except the ice in a food processor fitted with the steel blade or a blender and process until pureed. Add the ice cubes and process until the ice is almost completely pulverized and the mixture is frothy. Pour into chilled glasses.

Serves 4

HERBED SPA OMELET

292
CALORIES PER SERVING

An extra egg white adds volume to this omelet but be sure to use a free hand with the seasonings. To vary the flavor, use fresh tarragon, oregano, or mint, and don't neglect the white pepper.

- 1 large egg
- 2 egg whites
- ¼ cup skim milk
  Freshly ground white pepper
  Pinch of vegetable seasoning
- ½ teaspoon chopped fresh thyme
- ½ teaspoon chopped Italian parsley
- ½ teaspoon chopped fresh basil
- ½ teaspoon snipped fresh chives or chopped scallion greens
- 1 teaspoon unsalted butter
  Fresh thyme sprig

- 1 slice chewy whole-grain bread
- 1 teaspoon fruit-only preserves

Preheat the broiler.

In a small bowl, whisk together the egg, egg whites, milk, pepper, and vegetable seasoning to taste, thyme, parsley, basil, and chives until well blended.

Spray a 6- or 7-inch omelet pan with a heatproof handle with vegetable cooking spray. Add the butter to the pan and place over moderate heat until the butter is bubbly. Pour the omelet mixture into the pan and cook until partially set, about 2 minutes, stirring once or twice.

Transfer the pan to the broiler and broil until the omelet is puffed and lightly golden, 1½ to 2 minutes. With a spatula, loosen the edges of the omelet, fold it into thirds, and slide it onto a warmed plate. Top with a thyme sprig.

While the omelet is cooking, toast the bread. Serve the toast and preserves with the omelet.

Serves 1

STEAMED VEGETABLES WITH RED BASMATI RICE

275
CALORIES PER SERVING

Basmati is the aristocrat of Indian long-grain rice—fluffy, tender, and aromatic. Red basmati, a California hybrid, is a beautiful reddish-brown rice that is much crunchier than the original Indian variety and has a distinctive flavor reminiscent of popcorn. Its texture and color offset the steamed and raw vegetables in this robust lunch. If red basmati is unavailable, the Texas-grown brown Texmati is an excellent alternative, but be aware that it requires longer cooking.

- 1 cup red basmati rice
- 2 cups water
- 2 cups broccoli florets
- 2 cups cauliflower florets
- 2 cups carrots sliced ½ inch thick on the diagonal
- 2 cups celery sliced ½ inch thick on the diagonal
- 2 cups snow pea pods, ends trimmed and strings removed
- 2 cups bok choy sliced 1 inch thick
- 8 scallions
- 1 red bell pepper, julienned
- 8 radishes, well washed
  Pepper Peanut Dipping Sauce *or* **Sweet and Sour Dipping Sauce**

Put the rice in a small saucepan, add the water, and bring to a boil. Stir the rice, reduce the heat, and simmer, covered, for 15 minutes. Remove the pan from the heat and let the rice stand, covered, for 5 minutes.

While the rice is cooking, steam the vegetables. At the Spa we use a three-tiered Chinese bamboo steamer set over 1½ inches of boiling water in a wok. Place the broccoli, cauliflower, carrots, and celery in the first tier; place the snow peas and bok choy in the second tier; and place the scallions and bell peppers in the third tier. Cover the first tier, place it in the wok, and steam for 3 minutes. Lift the cover, stack the second tier on top, cover again, and steam for 1 minute. Lift the cover, stack the third tier, cover, and steam for 30 seconds. If you don't have a bamboo steamer, steam the vegetables individually or in as many batches as are manageable: 4½ to 5 minutes for the broccoli, cauliflower, carrots, and celery; 1½ to 2 minutes for the snow peas and bok choy; and ½ minute or so to take the chill off the scallions and bell pepper.

To serve, divide the rice among 4 heated plates and arrange the steamed vegetables around it. Garnish the plates with the radishes and pass the sauces separately.

Serves 4

PEPPER PEANUT DIPPING SAUCE

23

CALORIES PER TABLESPOON

This sauce is also very tasty served with raw vegetables, or use it as an alternative dressing for the Marco Polo Chicken and Pasta Salad (page 91).

 1 onion, chopped
 3 tablespoons unsalted chunky
   peanut butter
 1 tablespoon low-sodium soy sauce
 1 teaspoon hot red pepper flakes
 ½ cup skim milk

Spray a small saucepan with vegetable cooking spray, add the onion, and sauté it over moderate heat until translucent, about 5 to 6 minutes. Add the peanut butter, soy sauce, red pepper, and milk and heat well, stirring to blend. Transfer the mixture to a blender and puree. Reheat if necessary and serve hot.

Makes 1 cup

SWEET AND SOUR DIPPING SAUCE

15

CALORIES PER TABLESPOON

Omit the arrowroot, add a few drops of hot pepper sauce, and transform this into a barbecue basting sauce for chicken or strips of very lean pork.

 ½ cup low-sodium soy sauce
 ¼ cup rice wine vinegar
 2 tablespoons fresh lemon juice
 2 tablespoons apple juice concentrate
 2 tablespoons fruit-only apricot
   preserves
 1 tablespoon Dijon mustard
 2 tablespoons minced garlic
 2 tablespoons chopped shallots
 1½ teaspoons arrowroot dissolved in
   2 teaspoons cold water

Combine the soy sauce, vinegar, lemon juice, apple juice concentrate, preserves, mustard, garlic, and shallots in a small saucepan and bring to a boil over high heat. Add the arrowroot mixture and simmer just until the sauce is thickened and clear, about 1 minute. Serve warm or at room temperature.

Makes 1 cup

APRICOT MOUSSE

155

CALORIES PER SERVING

After the strong flavors and textures of steamed rice and vegetables, our apricot mousse is a cool and soothing finale. Make it in the morning so that it's perfectly chilled by lunchtime.

 1 cup unsulfured dried whole apricots
 ½ cup apricot juice or water
 ¼ cup plus 1 tablespoon fructose
 1 tablespoon lemon juice
 3 egg whites, at room temperature

In a nonreactive saucepan, combine the apricots, juice, and fructose and cook over low heat until the apricots are tender and have a marmalade consistency, about 10 to 15 minutes. Transfer the mixture to the bowl of a food processor fitted with the steel blade or to a blender and puree. Turn the apricot puree into a bowl and let cool to room temperature.

In a mixing bowl, beat the lemon juice and egg whites until the whites are stiff but not dry. Stir one-quarter of the whites into the apricot mixture, then fold in the rest. Turn the mousse into chilled goblets and refrigerate until cold.

Serves 4

DAY
2

DINNER

595
CALORIES

•

PORK TENDERLOIN ROASTED WITH
WHOLE GARLIC AND ROSEMARY

•

MASHED CELERIAC WITH
CHOPPED APPLE

•

BEET GREENS

•

PUMPKIN CHEESECAKE

•

PORK TENDERLOIN ROASTED WITH WHOLE GARLIC AND ROSEMARY

312
CALORIES PER SERVING

Pork, once a forbidden food because of its high fat content, has been transformed by health-conscious hog farmers into a white meat calorically comparable to veal and even richer in flavor. In this simple recipe, whole pork tenderloins are trimmed of all fat and packaged in foil with fresh herbs and elephant garlic, then cooked to juicy perfection. Even served with a boiled Red Bliss potato instead of the celeriac, this dish would be suitable for a Spa menu.

> 2 lean boneless pork tenderloins
> (about 8 ounces each)
> Ground coriander
> Vegetable seasoning
> Freshly ground black pepper
> ¼ cup extra-virgin olive oil
> 2 whole elephant garlic heads,
> unpeeled
> 6 large fresh rosemary sprigs
> 4 fresh thyme sprigs
> 2 bay leaves

Preheat the oven to 350° F.

Trim off any fat on the pork. Combine the coriander, vegetable seasoning, and black pepper to taste in a small bowl, and rub the pork all over with the mixture.

Cut 2 large squares of foil for each tenderloin and make 2 stacks of 2 layers each. Rub the top layer of foil with some of the oil. Rub the remaining oil over the pork and heads of garlic. Place the pork on the foil, put the garlic next to it, and arrange the herbs over the pork. Fold both layers of foil over and crimp the edges to seal, leaving some room for steam inside the packets.

Place the packets on a baking sheet and bake for 30 to 35 minutes. Remove the meat from the oven and insert an instant-read meat thermometer through the foil and into the pork. The thermometer should read 150° to 155° F. Leave the thermometer in the pork and let the meat stand for 10 minutes, during which it will continue to steam in the foil and eventually reach 160° F.

Open the foil packets and let the pork rest for 10 to 15 minutes longer. Cut the heads of garlic in half and cut off the root ends.

Cut the pork into ¼-inch slices and arrange on heated serving plates. Distribute the garlic among the plates and serve with the celeriac and beet greens.

Serves 4

MASHED CELERIAC WITH CHOPPED APPLE

178
CALORIES PER SERVING

As its name implies, celeriac is a celery-flavored root vegetable, still more popular in Europe than America. Using Yankee ingenuity, we have translated this typical French dish—a puree of celeriac and potato—into New Spa Food by cutting down on the butter and substituting skim milk for heavy cream. It is a great alternative to mashed potatoes, which it resembles.

> 2 large celery roots (about
> 1¾ pounds in all)
> 1 large all-purpose potato (about
> 8 ounces)
> Juice of 1 lemon
> 2 to 2½ cups apple juice
> 2 tablespoons unsalted butter
> Vegetable seasoning
> Freshly ground black pepper
> ½ cup evaporated skim milk (optional)
> 1 medium red apple

Peel the celery roots and potato and cut them into 1-inch cubes. (As you work, place the cubes in a bowl of cold water acidulated with the lemon juice to keep them from turning dark.) Drain the vegetables and place them in a medium saucepan. Add apple juice to cover and bring to a boil over high heat. Reduce the heat, cover the pan, and simmer the vegetables until they are tender but not overcooked, about 15 minutes.

Drain the vegetables, reserving the cooking liquid, place them in a mixing bowl, and mash them, either with a hand mixer or by putting them through a ricer. (Do not use a food processor, as this would make the puree gummy.)

Season the puree with butter and add vegetable seasoning and pepper to taste. Adjust the consistency by adding some of the reserved cooking liquid or, if you prefer a creamier dish, the evaporated milk. Transfer the mixture to the saucepan and reheat, beating the puree until it is fluffy.

Just before serving, cut the apple into quarters, remove the core, and cut the fruit into ½-inch dice. Serve the puree garnished with the apple.

Serves 4

BEET GREENS

3 0

CALORIES PER SERVING

Strongly flavored but not overpowering, beet greens are delicious with pork. Buy thin-ribbed beet tops that are fresh, clean, and dark green. Pass up any that are wilted or tough.

> 1 to 1½ pounds beet greens
> ½ to ¾ cup water seasoned with vegetable seasoning to taste
> Fresh lemon juice
> Freshly ground black pepper

Wash and trim the beet greens, discarding the stems and any greens that are wilted or yellowed. If the leaves are very large, cut them into pieces.

Heat a large heavy skillet over high heat and pour in just enough seasoned water to prevent the greens from scorching. When the water reaches a boil, add the greens and cook, stirring often, until the greens are wilted and just tender, 3 to 4 minutes. Do not overcook. Season with lemon juice and pepper to taste, drain slightly, and serve at once.

Serves 4

PUMPKIN CHEESECAKE

7 5

CALORIES PER SERVING

This recipe, which makes 12 irresistible servings, raises the eternal question: What to do with the leftovers? And the answer, of course, is freeze them or give them away—you'll find lots of willing takers. Don't be dismayed if the crust crumbles as you transfer the cheesecake from pie plate to serving plate; just spoon up the crumbs and sprinkle them over the cake.

CRUST

> 2 to 3 slices whole wheat bread
> 2 tablespoons unsweetened apple juice concentrate
> ¼ teaspoon ground cinnamon

FILLING

> 16 ounces 1% fat cottage cheese
> 1 15-ounce can unsweetened pumpkin puree
> ½ cup soft tofu
> 1 large egg
> 2 egg whites
> 1 tablespoon whole wheat pastry flour
> ¼ cup fructose
> ¼ cup unsweetened apple juice concentrate
> 1 teaspoon ground cinnamon
> ¼ teaspoon ground allspice
> ¼ teaspoon freshly grated nutmeg
> 1 teaspoon vanilla extract

Preheat the oven to 350° F. Spray a 10-inch pie plate with vegetable cooking spray.

To make the crust, tear the bread into pieces, place them in a food processor fitted with the steel blade, and process into fine crumbs. Add the apple juice concentrate and cinnamon and process to blend the ingredients. Pat the crumb mixture evenly into the pie plate and bake the crust for 10 minutes. Remove the plate from the oven and let the crust cool. Leave the oven on.

For the filling, place the cottage cheese, pumpkin puree, tofu, egg, egg whites, flour, fructose, apple juice concentrate, cinnamon, allspice, nutmeg, and vanilla in the bowl of the food processor and process with the steel blade until the mixture is a smooth puree. Pour the filling into the crust and bake for 40 to 45 minutes, until set. Let the cheesecake cool on a rack before slicing.

Serves 12

DAY
3

BREAKFAST

325

CALORIES

•

SPA SCRAMBLED EGGS

•

OATMEAL AND RAISIN MUFFINS

•

DECAFFEINATED COFFEE
OR TEA

•

LUNCH

537

CALORIES

•

GREENS WITH CUCUMBER AND
MARINATED BEET

•

NORWICH SEAFOOD CHOWDER

•

BROWN RICE PUDDING

•

SPA SCRAMBLED EGGS

145
CALORIES PER SERVING

Pouring the beaten eggs through a strainer to remove any solid bits of albumen before adding any herbs or seasonings ensures smooth, silky scrambled eggs and omelets.

    4 large eggs
    8 egg whites
      Freshly ground black or
      white pepper
    4 teaspoons unsalted butter or
      margarine
    4 fresh chervil sprigs

In a mixing bowl whisk together the eggs and egg whites until well combined. Pour the mixture through a strainer into another bowl and stir in the pepper.

Spray a nonstick skillet or omelet pan with vegetable cooking spray and heat over moderate heat. Add the butter and let it melt. Reduce the heat, pour in the eggs, and cook them gently, stirring with a wooden spoon or rubber spatula until soft curds form. When the eggs are cooked to your taste, distribute them among 4 heated plates, garnish with chervil, and serve at once.

Serves 4

OATMEAL AND RAISIN MUFFINS

180
CALORIES PER MUFFIN

Like our pumpkin and bran muffins, these freeze very well and can be individually reheated in a toaster oven or microwave. Served with a bowl of fresh fruit and yogurt, they make a lovely and somewhat less caloric breakfast.

    1 cup rolled oats
    ⅔ cup raisins
    1 cup buttermilk
    1 cup whole wheat pastry flour
    1 teaspoon baking soda
    ¼ cup oat bran
    ⅓ cup safflower oil
    ⅓ cup packed dark brown sugar
    1 large egg

Place the oats and raisins in a mixing bowl, then stir in the buttermilk. Let the mixture stand for 20 to 30 minutes.

Preheat the oven to 375° F. Line a muffin pan with paper cupcake liners.

In a bowl, combine the flour, baking soda, and bran. In a large mixing bowl, beat the oil and sugar until well blended. Add the egg and blend well. Stir the buttermilk and flour mixtures alternately into the egg mixture, mixing well after each addition.

Spoon the batter into the muffin tins and bake for about 30 minutes, or until golden brown. Let cool on a rack.

Makes 12 muffins

GREENS WITH CUCUMBER AND MARINATED BEET

126
CALORIES PER SERVING

An aromatic, orange-flavored dressing and finely diced beets make this a pretty and refreshing salad. Beets, depending on their age and size, cook slowly or very slowly, which accounts for the span of the cooking time given in the recipe.

    1 medium or 2 small beets
    ½ teaspoon grated orange zest
    1 tablespoon fresh orange juice
    1 tablespoon red wine vinegar
    2 tablespoons extra-virgin olive oil
    5 tablespoons mineral water
      Freshly ground black pepper
    2 quarts mixed greens
    1 Belgian endive
    ¼ hothouse cucumber, thinly sliced

Trim off all but 1½ to 2 inches of the beet stem (do not cut off the root end) and scrub the beet with a vegetable brush. Place in a saucepan with cold water to cover and bring to a boil over high heat. Cook the beet until it is tender, 25 to 50 minutes.

Meanwhile, in a small bowl combine the orange zest, orange juice, vinegar, oil, mineral water, and a generous grinding of pepper. Whisk well.

Drain the beet. When it is cool enough to handle, cut off the stem end and slip off the skin. Trim away the root and cut the beet into ¼-inch dice; you should have about ¾ cup. Add the beet to the vinaigrette, cover, and marinate for several hours or overnight.

To assemble the salad, toss the greens and endive together in a bowl to mix, then spread them out on 4 salad plates. Fan out the cucumber slices on each plate and spoon the beet and dressing over the greens.

Serves 4

NORWICH SEAFOOD CHOWDER

195
CALORIES PER SERVING

Light but filling, this is one of the best and healthiest chowders you'll ever taste —clams, mussels, scallops, and cod fillets cooked at *à point* in fish stock flavored with wine, aromatic vegetables, and tomatoes. Don't be daunted by what seems to be a vast number of ingredients. If you have fish or vegetable stock in your freezer, fine—but water will do very nicely. The recipe can be prepared through cooking the potatoes a few hours in advance, so you'll need only 10 minutes to reheat the chowder and cook the seafood. Whole wheat grainary bread, cut in thin strips and toasted, makes a nice garnish.

   1 tablespoon extra-virgin olive oil
   2 teaspoons minced garlic
   1 small onion, chopped
   1 celery stalk, cut into ¼-inch dice
   1 carrot, peeled and cut into
      ⅛-inch slices
   2 scallions, cut into ¼-inch slices
   3 fresh thyme sprigs
2½ cups Fish Stock (page 142),
      High-Potassium Vegetable Stock
      (page 143), or water
   1 medium potato, cut into ¼-inch dice
   1 cup dry white wine
   1 cup canned low-sodium tomatoes,
      undrained
   8 littleneck clams, scrubbed
   8 mussels, scrubbed and debearded
   8 sea scallops
   4 ounces cod or scrod fillets
      Freshly cracked black pepper
      Vegetable seasoning
      Chopped fresh parsley or chervil

In a large soup kettle, heat the oil over moderate heat. Add the garlic, onion, celery, carrot, scallions, and thyme and sauté until the vegetables are soft, about 6 to 8 minutes. Add the stock and potato and bring to a boil. Reduce the heat, cover, and cook until the potato is soft, about 12 minutes.

Add the wine and tomatoes, return the soup to a boil, then add the clams and mussels. Cover the kettle and cook until the shellfish have opened, about 4 to 5 minutes. Add the scallops and fish, reduce the heat, and simmer the soup until the fish is cooked, about 5 minutes. Add pepper and vegetable seasoning to taste, and discard any shellfish that have not opened.

Remove the clams and mussels from their shells, if you wish, and serve the chowder in heated soup bowls, decorated with parsley.

Serves 4

BROWN RICE PUDDING

216
CALORIES PER SERVING

Should there ever be a Michelin *Guide to Spa Food,* this homey dessert will definitely be worth a detour. It's a more substantial and satisfying version of the usual white-rice pudding.

   1 quart skim milk
   1 cup cooked brown rice
   ¼ cup raisins
   1 cinnamon stick
   1 teaspoon vanilla extract
   1 teaspoon grated lemon zest
1½ tablespoons cornstarch
   2 tablespoons cold water
   1 large egg
   2 egg whites
      Freshly grated nutmeg

Preheat the oven to 350° F.

Combine the milk, rice, and raisins in the top of a double boiler and mix well. Set the pan over simmering water and scald the milk. Add the cinnamon stick, vanilla, and lemon zest. In a cup, combine the cornstarch and cold water; stir the mixture into the rice mixture. Continue cooking until the liquid is slightly thickened.

Meanwhile, beat the egg and egg whites in a small bowl. Ladle about ¼ cup of the hot rice mixture into the eggs, beating constantly. Beat in another ¼ cup of the rice mixture, then stir the egg mixture into the remaining rice mixture. Stir constantly over simmering water for 3 to 5 minutes; do not let the mixture boil or the eggs will curdle. Remove the cinnamon stick.

Turn the pudding into a shallow 9 x 12-inch oval baking dish and bake for 10 minutes, or until set. Serve slightly warm or chilled, sprinkled with nutmeg.

Serves 4

DINNER

662 CALORIES

•

OSSO BUCO

•

MILLET WITH PARMESAN CHEESE

•

BROCCOLI DI RAPE SAUTÉED
WITH GARLIC

•

CANTALOUPE SORBET

DAY 3

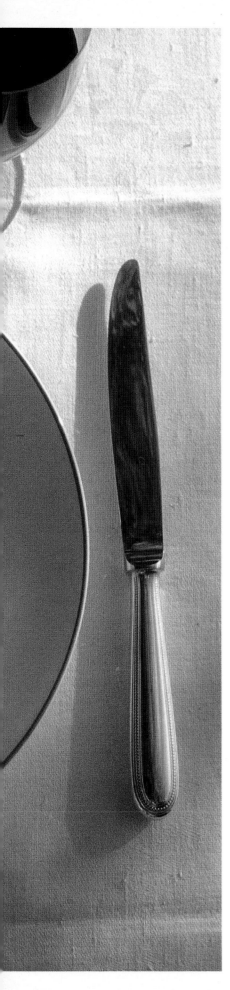

OSSO BUCO

371

CALORIES PER SERVING

A Milanese specialty, osso buco is made
of succulent veal shanks braised in a
white-wine tomato sauce and finished
with gremolata, a mixture of chopped
parsley, lemon zest, anchovy, and garlic.
The dish tastes even better if it's made a
day ahead.

   ¼ cup safflower oil
   1 large onion, finely chopped
   1 teaspoon minced garlic
   ½ cup whole wheat flour
      Vegetable seasoning
      Freshly ground black pepper
   4 2-inch pieces veal shank (about
      1¼ pounds in all)
   1 cup dry white wine
   ½ cup Low-Sodium Veal Stock
      (page 143) or Low-Sodium Chicken
      Stock (page 141)
   1 small carrot, peeled and cut into
      ¼-inch dice
   1½ cups low-sodium canned tomatoes,
      chopped, with juice
   1 bay leaf

GREMOLATA
   2 tablespoons chopped Italian parsley
   1½ tablespoons grated lemon zest
   1 anchovy fillet, roughly chopped
   ½ teaspoon minced garlic

   Heat the oil over moderate heat in
a heavy sauté pan or saucepan. Add the
onion and garlic and sauté until they
are translucent but not browned, about
5 minutes.

   In a shallow bowl, combine the
flour with vegetable seasoning and
pepper to taste and dredge the veal in
the mixture. Shake off the excess flour
and add the veal to the pan. Raise the
heat to moderately high and brown the
shanks on both sides. Add 2 to 3
tablespoons of the flour mixture to the
pan and cook, stirring constantly, for 3
to 4 minutes, or until the flour is
cooked. Stir in the wine and stock and
cook, stirring often, until thickened.
Add the carrots, tomatoes with their
juice, and bay leaf, cover the pan, and
reduce the heat so that the liquid is at a
steady simmer. Cook 35 to 40 minutes,
or until the veal is tender, turning the
shanks occasionally and adding more
stock or water if necessary.

   To make the gremolata, combine
the parsley, lemon zest, anchovy, and
garlic. Serve the shanks on heated
plates, topped with the gremolata and
accompanied by the millet and broccoli
di rape.

Serves 4

MILLET WITH PARMESAN CHEESE

119

CALORIES PER SERVING

Pale yellow, with a mild taste and a nice
crunch, millet is an ideal backdrop for
the highly flavored osso buco. If millet is
not available, or if cornmeal appeals
more to you, simmer ½ cup of stone-
ground cornmeal in 2½ cups of water for
about 30 minutes, stirring often, then
combine it with the Parmesan, olive oil,
and pepper for a tasty polenta side dish.

   ½ cup millet
   1 cup water
   2 tablespoons freshly grated
      Parmesan cheese
   1 tablespoon extra-virgin olive oil
      Freshly ground black pepper

   Place the millet in a sieve, wash it
under cold running water, and drain
well. Put the millet in a small skillet and
dry roast over moderate heat, stirring
constantly, until the grain takes on a
light tan color, about 2 to 3 minutes.
   Bring the water to a boil in a small
saucepan, add the millet, and lower the
heat. Cover the pan and simmer the
millet until tender, 15 to 20 minutes.
Add the Parmesan, oil, and black
pepper to taste and toss to mix.

Serves 4

BROCCOLI DI RAPE SAUTÉED WITH GARLIC

90
CALORIES PER SERVING

If you haven't yet tried broccoli di rape, don't wait a moment longer. Related to broccoli but more robust in flavor and texture, this pungent and slightly bitter vegetable is used often in Tuscan and Sicilian cooking. Try this recipe, without the sesame seeds and with a little more oil, tossed with whole wheat pasta shells or penne and sprinkled with some freshly grated Parmesan cheese.

1½ pounds broccoli di rape
1 tablespoon extra-virgin olive oil
1 tablespoon minced garlic
Spicy vegetable seasoning
Lemon pepper
1 tablespoon toasted sesame seeds

Cut the tough stem end from the broccoli di rape, then cut the vegetable into rough 1-inch lengths. Wash the broccoli well, leaving some water adhering to the leaves.

Heat a sauté pan over moderate heat, spray the pan with vegetable cooking spray, and add the oil and garlic. Cook the garlic for 1 to 2 minutes, but do not let it brown. Add the broccoli and toss it with the garlic. Cover the pan and let the broccoli steam for 6 to 10 minutes, depending on how crisp you want it. Stir from time to time, and add a spoonful or two of water if the broccoli sticks to the bottom of the pan.

Season to taste with spicy vegetable seasoning and lemon pepper. Serve sprinkled with toasted sesame seeds.

Serves 4

CANTALOUPE SORBET

82
CALORIES PER SERVING

Cool and pretty, peach-colored cantaloupe sorbet makes a fresh-tasting finish to an intensely flavored meal.

1 large cantaloupe
½ cup fresh orange juice
½ teaspoon lemon extract
1 tablespoon honey (optional)
½ cup seedless green grapes

Cut the cantaloupe flesh into chunks, discarding the seeds and rind, and puree the flesh in a food processor fitted with the steel blade. You should have about 2½ cups of puree. Add the orange juice and lemon extract and process until mixed. Taste the puree and add the honey if the mixture is not sweet enough.

Chill the puree and freeze it in an electric or hand-cranked ice-cream maker, following the manufacturer's instructions.

To make the sorbet in your freezer, transfer the mixture to a bowl and place in the freezer. When the liquid has frozen solid, about 2 to 3 hours, remove it from the freezer and, with a fork, break it into large chunks. Place the chunks in a food processor and process with the steel blade until smooth and creamy. Return it to the bowl and freeze for at least 30 minutes more.

To serve, distribute the grapes among 4 glass dessert coupes and place scoops of sorbet over them. Serve at once.

Makes 1 quart, serving 4

SORBET VARIATIONS

Virtually any fruit puree or fruit juice can be made into a marvelous sorbet in your freezer. Raspberries, strawberries, cranberries, red currants, cherries, kiwi fruit, passion fruit, rhubarb, cantaloupes, apples, peaches, and apricots all work well, but just about any fruit you find at your greengrocer or farmer's market will do.

The trick to making a great sorbet with a smooth, firm texture that is not granular is achieving a proper balance of sugar to liquids. Too much sugar and the sorbet will never freeze completely; too little and it will be rock hard when frozen. At the Spa we use granulated fructose to add sweetness to the sorbet.

Start with 1 cup of pureed fruit. (Depending on the ripeness of the fruit, you may want to sweeten the puree slightly with a pinch or two of fructose and a squeeze of lemon juice.) To the puree, add up to 2 cups of warm water, or fruit juice for a more intensely flavored (and caloric) sorbet. This is your base.

Next, try this chef's trick to see if it will freeze properly: float a whole raw egg (it should be well washed) in the mixture. If the mixture has the proper sugar content the tip of the eggshell that shows above the surface of the mixture will be about the diameter of a dime. If the egg does not rise to the surface of the mixture, you will need to add more fructose, up to 4 tablespoons, to achieve the right sweetness balance. If, on the other hand, the egg protrudes too far from the mixture, you must thin it with more warm water or additional fruit juice. Because different fruits have different densities of sugar, you will have to experiment with the proportions each time.

This may sound complicated, but in practice it is quite easy, and once you have mastered the technique, there is no limit to the variations you can devise.

D A Y

4

BREAKFAST

306
CALORIES
•
HERBAL TEA
•
BIRCHER MUESLI
WITH YOGURT
•

LUNCH

470
CALORIES
•
VEGETABLE LASAGNA
•
ROMAINE SALAD
WITH CREAMY
ITALIAN DRESSING
•
GRAPES
•

HERBAL TEAS

1
CALORIE PER SERVING

Although a cup of tea contains less caffeine than a comparable amount of coffee, many people prefer to avoid caffeine whenever possible. Fortunately, there are so many flavorful and full-bodied herbal teas to choose from, making the switch from caffeinated tea to a herbal variety or blend is hardly a sacrifice. Chamomile, lemongrass, rose hip, peppermint, and hibiscus are some of the most common, but search out interesting blends that incorporate spice and fruit flavors, seeds like fennel, and herbs like lavender. Japanese food shops also carry some interesting tealike beverages made from toasted grains, such as barley, which have a substantial, hearty flavor and aroma.

In addition, you can perk up a cup of herbal tea with one or more of the following:

- Flavored honey, such as lavender, orange blossom, blueberry, or wild flower
- Maple sugar granules, made from maple syrup boiled to the point of crystallization
- Fruit syrups in any number of flavors
- Citrus peel or a slice of fruit, including orange, lime, or tangerine, as well as the ubiquitous lemon
- Fresh herbs, especially mint and lavender wands
- Cinnamon sticks, particularly good with spicy, fruit-flavored teas
- Crystallized ginger, for a delicate, elegant hint of flavor

To make a perfect pot of herbal tea, pour very hot (not boiling) water over 5 generous teaspoons of loose leaves or 5 tea bags and steep for at least 3 minutes to allow the flavor to develop. Strain into individual teacups or discard tea bags, and add one or more of the garnishes above to each cup.

Serves 4

BIRCHER MUESLI

305
CALORIES PER SERVING

A European breakfast staple, this blend of rolled oats, crunchy sunflower seeds, and fresh and dried fruits steeps overnight in honey-and-vanilla-flavored milk. Use the next morning, before the fruits lose all their goodness and flavor and the cereal becomes soggy. Diced orange and apple complete the meal, which is high in protein, B vitamins, calcium, and fiber. The yogurt adds 37 calories per serving.

- 1⅓ cups rolled oats
- ⅓ cup toasted sunflower seeds
- ⅓ cup raisins
- ⅓ cup sliced strawberries
- ⅓ cup blueberries
- 2 cups skim milk
- ½ teaspoon freshly grated nutmeg
- Scant 1 teaspoon vanilla extract
- 2 teaspoons honey
- 1 small apple
- 1 navel orange
- Strawberries for garnish
- ⅓ cup nonfat plain yogurt

In a large bowl, combine the oats, sunflower seeds, raisins, sliced strawberries, blueberries, milk, nutmeg, vanilla, and honey and mix well. Cover the bowl with plastic wrap and refrigerate overnight.

Just before serving, core the apple (but do not peel) and cut into dice. Peel the orange and cut into dice. Add the apple and orange to the muesli. Mix well, distribute among 4 cereal bowls, and garnish with strawberries. Serve the yogurt separately.

Serves 4

VEGETABLE LASAGNA

345
CALORIES PER SERVING

Everyone loves lasagna. This recipe takes a little extra time to make, but it can be assembled well ahead of time—even the night before—and baked before serving. The recipe can also be doubled or tripled to serve to an appreciative crowd.

- 2 whole wheat pasta sheets (page 144)
- 1 pound eggplant, unpeeled, cut into ¼-inch lengthwise slices
- 1 pound zucchini, cut into ¼-inch lengthwise slices
- 2 cups sliced mushrooms
- 1 cup low-fat cottage cheese
- ½ cup part-skim ricotta cheese
- 1 tablespoon freshly grated Parmesan cheese
- ½ cup shredded part-skim or imported buffalo mozzarella
- 2 egg whites
- 1 teaspoon minced garlic
- 2 tablespoons chopped fresh basil
- 1 tablespoon fresh oregano
- Vegetable seasoning
- Freshly ground white pepper
- 2 cups Red Wine Tomato Sauce (page 141)
- ¼ cup freshly grated Asiago cheese

Bring a large pot of water to a boil, add the lasagna, and cook until just al dente. Drain the noodles, spread them out on a lightly oiled plate, and reserve.

While the noodles are cooking, steam the eggplant and then the zucchini for 2 to 3 minutes each, just until each vegetable is lightly cooked but not soft or limp. Turn the steamed vegetables into a bowl of cold water to stop the cooking, drain, and set each aside separately.

Spray a medium skillet with vegetable cooking spray and place over moderate heat. Add the mushrooms and sauté 4 to 5 minutes. Reserve the mushrooms.

To make the cheese filling, place the cottage cheese, ricotta, Parmesan, mozzarella, and egg whites in a food processor and blend until smooth. Transfer the mixture to a bowl, stir in the garlic, basil, oregano, and vegetable seasoning and white pepper to taste, and mix well.

Preheat the oven to 350° F.

To assemble the lasagna, spray an 8-inch square or round baking dish with vegetable spray. Spread a generous ⅓ cup tomato sauce on the bottom of the pan and cover with half the pasta. Layer as follows: one-third of the mushrooms, one-third of the cheese mixture, ⅓ cup tomato sauce, all the eggplant slices, half the remaining mushrooms, half the remaining cheese mixture, ⅓ cup tomato sauce, all the zucchini, the remaining mushrooms, the remaining cheese mixture, ⅓ cup tomato sauce, the remaining lasagna noodles, the remaining tomato sauce, and finally the Asiago, sprinkled over the top.

Cover the dish and bake the lasagna for 35 to 40 minutes. Remove the cover and bake 10 minutes more, or until the top is browned. Let the dish stand for about 10 minutes, then cut into quarters and serve.

Serves 4

ROMAINE SALAD WITH CREAMY ITALIAN DRESSING

6 7
CALORIES PER SERVING

My father always ate plain romaine lettuce after dinner to "sweep the stomach." We've improved on this with a standout yogurt-tarragon dressing. You'll need only half the dressing for the salad, but the rest will keep for up to 4 days, refrigerated in a tightly covered container.

1 large head romaine

CREAMY ITALIAN DRESSING
  6 tablespoons low-fat plain yogurt
  5 tablespoons tarragon vinegar
  2 tablespoons extra-virgin olive oil
  2 teaspoons Dijon mustard
  1½ teaspoons chopped fresh tarragon
  1½ teaspoons chopped fresh basil
  1½ teaspoons chopped Italian parsley
  Freshly ground white pepper

Separate the head of romaine into leaves. Wash the leaves and pat dry. Tear them into bite-size pieces and arrange on individual salad plates.

To make the dressing, whisk together the yogurt, vinegar, oil, mustard, tarragon, basil, and parsley in a small bowl. Stir in pepper to taste. To serve, spoon 2 tablespoons of dressing over each portion of salad, or pass the dressing in a small pitcher.

Serves 4

FRESH FRUIT

5 5   t o   8 0
CALORIES PER SERVING

Almost any raw fruit, except perhaps grapefruit, lemon, or banana, is a happy choice after a lasagna lunch. For this occasion we served 1-cup portions of red, black, and green seedless grapes, but here are approximate calorie counts for some other fruits that would complement the meal nicely:
- 2 medium figs, 80 calories
- 1 cup Concord, Delaware, or Niagara grapes, 70 calories
- ¾ cup Malaga, Muscat, or Thompson grapes, 80 calories
- 3 apricots, 54 calories
- 1 medium orange, in sections, 64 calories
- 1 medium nectarine, 88 calories
- 1 medium peach, peeled, 38 calories
- 1 bosc pear, sliced, 85 calories
- ½ d'angou pear, sliced, 60 calories
- 1 cup pineapple, 80 calories
- 1 cup strawberries, 55 calories

D A Y

4

D I N N E R

6 4 7
CALORIES

•

FRESH AND DRIED
MUSHROOM
BUTTERMILK SOUP

•

BROCHETTE OF CHICKEN

•

COUSCOUS OR
SPICY CURRIED LENTILS

•

MINTED YOGURT SAUCE

•

POACHED PEARS WITH
PLUM PUREE

•

FRESH AND DRIED MUSHROOM BUTTERMILK SOUP

175
CALORIES PER SERVING

Onions, wild mushrooms, and sour cream are used together in many Eastern European soups and stews. We've edited this traditional Polish recipe to fit the Spa menu by eliminating the butter, whole milk, and sour cream, a combination rich in calcium and disastrously high in cholesterol. In their stead we've used evaporated skim milk and buttermilk, resulting in a slightly tart flavor that plays well against the robust mushrooms. Dried morels tend to retain sand in their many crevices, so wash them thoroughly under running water before you cook them.

½ ounce dried cèpe mushrooms
½ ounce dried morel or porcini mushrooms
3 cups Low-Sodium Veal Stock (page 143) or High-Potassium Vegetable Stock (page 143)
1 cup finely chopped onions
2 tablespoons low-sodium soy sauce
3 or 4 cultivated mushrooms, chopped (about ½ cup)
½ cup whole wheat flour
1 teaspoon fructose
½ cup water
1 cup buttermilk
½ cup evaporated skim milk
Paprika (optional)
2 mushrooms (any type), halved, for garnish

Wash the cèpes and morels well under running water and place in a 2-quart saucepan. Add the stock and bring to a boil over high heat. Reduce the heat and simmer the mushrooms slowly, uncovered, for 20 to 30 minutes, or until they are reconstituted and tender. Strain the liquid and reserve the stock and mushrooms separately.

Rinse out the saucepan and return the stock to it. Add the onions, soy sauce, and chopped cultivated mushrooms. Bring to a boil, reduce the heat, and slowly simmer, uncovered, for 10 minutes.

Slice the cèpes and morels and rinse them under running water to remove any remaining sand or hidden sediment. Place the mushrooms in a food processor fitted with the steel blade, pour in the stock mixture, and puree.

Return the soup to the saucepan and bring back to a simmer over moderate heat. Combine the flour, fructose, and water in a small bowl. Hold a sieve over the simmering soup and slowly pour in the flour mixture. Cook for 2 to 3 minutes, stirring occasionally. Stir in the buttermilk and evaporated skim milk and return the soup to a simmer, but do not let it boil.

Serve the soup in heated bowls sprinkled with paprika, if desired, and topped with a mushroom half.

Serves 4

BROCHETTE OF CHICKEN

160
CALORIES PER SERVING

Brochettes are a good choice for an impressive-looking meal that can be assembled quickly. Try turkey breast, shrimp, or swordfish steak instead of chicken, and thread a few raw mushrooms, cherry tomatoes, and onion chunks among the other vegetables.

½ yellow bell pepper
½ red bell pepper
1 carrot, peeled
1 medium zucchini
1 yellow squash
8 mushroom caps
4 boneless, skinless chicken breast halves (about 1 pound in all)
¾ cup Spa Vinaigrette (page 140)

Soak 4 bamboo skewers in water.
Core the bell peppers and cut into 1-inch pieces. Cut the carrot on the diagonal into 1-inch pieces. Bring a pot of water to a boil. Place the bell pepper pieces in a strainer, lower into the boiling water, and blanch until they are no longer raw but still crisp. Drain and cool the peppers in a bowl of cold water. Blanch, drain, and cool the carrot pieces.

Trim the zucchini and yellow squash and cut on the diagonal into 1-inch slices. Trim the stems from the mushrooms and halve. Cut each half chicken breast half into 5 pieces.

Thread each skewer with the chicken, zucchini, bell peppers, carrot, yellow squash, and mushrooms. Place the skewers in a shallow pan, pour the vinaigrette over them, and marinate for 30 to 60 minutes, turning the skewers 2 or 3 times.

Prepare a charcoal grill or preheat the broiler.

Remove the brochettes from the marinade and grill or broil, turning often and basting with the marinade, for about 10 minutes, or until the chicken is cooked. Place the brochettes on heated dinner plates and serve with couscous, lentils, and minted yogurt sauce.

Serves 4

COUSCOUS

120

CALORIES PER SERVING

Couscous is the national dish of Morocco and has become a household staple. In authentic Moroccan cuisine, the raw semolina pellets are washed, drained, and steamed, usually over an aromatic stew, or *tagine*. Next, it is spread out in a pan to dry for about 10 minutes; it then steams a second time. For our purposes, instant couscous is a sensible and delicious choice.

1½ cups Low-Sodium Chicken Stock (page 141) or water
1 cup instant couscous
Vegetable seasoning

Bring the stock to a boil in a medium saucepan over high heat. Stir in the couscous, reduce the heat, and cover. Cook for 3 to 5 minutes, or until all of the stock is absorbed and the couscous is fluffy. Stir with a fork and add vegetable seasoning to taste.

Serves 4 to 6

MINTED YOGURT SAUCE

25

CALORIES PER SERVING

Use this refreshing blend as a dressing for thinly sliced cucumbers, radishes, and scallions. Or double the amount of yogurt for a refreshing warm weather soup.

1 cup nonfat plain yogurt
1 tablespoon chopped fresh mint

At least 1 hour before serving, blend the yogurt and mint in a bowl. Cover and let stand in the refrigerator.

Serves 4

SPICY CURRIED LENTILS

135

CALORIES PER SERVING

One of my mother's favorites, the earthy flavor of the lentils in this dish is offset by the mildly spicy curry powder and cumin. A tablespoon of vegetable oil and 2 teaspoons of lemon juice, added once the lentils have cooled, will turn this recipe into a fine hot-weather side dish. Or spoon the lentils into a pita bread with very thin slices of lean beef.

1 onion
1 carrot, peeled
1 teaspoon chopped garlic
1 16-ounce can low-sodium tomatoes, drained and juice reserved
½ cup lentils
1 cup High-Potassium Vegetable Stock (page 143) or water
1 bay leaf
1 teaspoon curry powder
1 teaspoon dried thyme
½ teaspoon ground cumin

Chop the onion and carrot and put them in a medium saucepan with the garlic and reserved tomato juice. Place over medium-low heat and cook until the onion is translucent, about 4 minutes.

Meanwhile, chop the tomatoes and rinse and pick over the lentils. Add the remaining ingredients to the onion mixture and bring to a boil. Lower the heat until the mixture simmers, cover, and cook until the lentils are tender, about 30 minutes. Check once or twice to make sure the liquid has not all been absorbed, adding more if necessary.

Serves 4

POACHED PEARS WITH PLUM PUREE

160

CALORIES PER SERVING

Poached pears, standing upright in a pool of fruit puree, are a serious-looking dessert. Luckily, they're simple to make. The puree in this instance is made with plums, but you can also use raspberries.

POACHED PEARS
5 to 6 cups apple juice
2 cinnamon sticks
4 small d'anjou pears

PLUM PUREE
8 quartered and pitted Italian or Santa Rosa plums
¼ cup water
¼ cup apple juice
1 to 2 tablespoons fructose

Place 5 cups of the apple juice in a medium saucepan. Add the cinnamon sticks and bring to a boil over high heat. Peel the pears and add them to the saucepan. Add enough additional juice to cover the pears completely. Reduce the heat, cover the pan, and simmer until the pears are tender but not mushy, about 10 to 15 minutes. Remove the lid and let the pears cool in the poaching liquid. Chill the pears in the liquid.

Meanwhile, prepare the plum puree. Place the plums, water, and apple juice in a medium saucepan and bring to a boil. Reduce the heat, cover the pan, and simmer until the plums are soft and the liquid is syrupy, being careful not to burn the plums. Transfer the mixture to a food processor and puree, then put the puree through a sieve to remove any remaining bits of skin. Add fructose to taste, depending on the sweetness of the plums. Chill the puree.

To serve, spoon the puree onto 4 chilled dessert plates and place a pear upright in the center of each.

Serves 4

D A Y

5

B R E A K F A S T

350
CALORIES

•

CHEESE BLINTZES WITH
BLUEBERRY SAUCE

•

DECAFFEINATED COFFEE OR TEA

•

L U N C H

4 9 6
CALORIES

•

MISO SOUP

•

MARCO POLO CHICKEN AND
PASTA SALAD

•

COLD SLICED ORANGES IN
GRAND MARNIER SAUCE

•

CHEESE BLINTZES WITH BLUEBERRY SAUCE

350
CALORIES PER SERVING

A beloved tradition in Jewish dairy cookery, blintzes are basically crêpes filled with cottage cheese and served with fruit sauce or sometimes preserves. Blintzes may be eaten at any time of day —or night. The crêpes, sometimes called blintze skins, can be made weeks in advance and frozen, then defrosted in the refrigerator overnight.

BLINTZE SKINS
- 1 large egg
- 2 egg whites
- 1 cup skim milk
- 1 tablespoon safflower oil
- ½ teaspoon fructose
- ½ teaspoon vanilla extract
- ¾ cup whole wheat pastry flour
- ¼ cup all-purpose flour
- 1 teaspoon ground cinnamon

FILLING
- 2 cups low-fat cottage cheese
- 1 teaspoon ground cinnamon
- ½ teaspoon vanilla extract
- 1 teaspoon grated orange zest

BLUEBERRY SAUCE
- 1 pint fresh or unsweetened frozen blueberries
- ¾ cup unsweetened apple juice
- 2 tablespoons arrowroot dissolved in 2 tablespoons cold water

To make the blintze skins, put the egg, egg whites, milk, oil, fructose, and vanilla in a blender jar or the bowl of a food processor fitted with the steel blade and blend until the mixture is smooth. Add the flours and cinnamon and blend until the batter is smooth. Cover the batter and refrigerate for at least 1 hour or overnight.

Spray a nonstick 8-inch crêpe pan with vegetable cooking spray and place over moderately high heat. Ladle about 2 tablespoons of the batter into the pan and swirl the pan to distribute the batter evenly over the bottom. Cook the skin until it is lightly browned, about 30 seconds, then, using a small spatula or your fingers, turn the blintze skin over to brown for another 3 to 4 seconds. Place the skin on a piece of wax paper and continue making blintze skins, placing wax paper between the layers.

The blintze skins can be used immediately or cooled, wrapped in plastic wrap and then foil, and frozen for up to 3 months.

To make the cheese filling, put the cottage cheese, cinnamon, vanilla, and orange zest in the bowl of a food processor fitted with the steel blade and process until smooth.

Preheat the oven to 350° F. Line a baking sheet with parchment paper.

To assemble the blintzes, place 8 skins on a flat surface and spoon about 2 tablespoons of filling 1 inch from the lower edge of each skin. Turn up the bottom edge of the skin, fold in the sides, and roll up the blintze. Place them seam side down on the baking sheet and bake the blintzes for 10 to 15 minutes, or until they are heated through.

Meanwhile, place the blueberries and apple juice in a medium saucepan, bring to a boil over high heat, then reduce the heat and simmer the fruit for 5 minutes, uncovered. Stir in the arrowroot mixture and cook until the sauce is thickened and clear, stirring constantly. Keep the sauce warm, but do not let it come to a simmer again.

Spoon some of the blueberry sauce on 4 plates. Place 2 blintzes on each plate and spoon the remaining sauce over them. Serve at once.

Serves 4

MISO SOUP

48
CALORIES PER SERVING

Miso, fermented soy bean paste, is a staple of Japanese cookery, prized for its flavor, aroma, and high protein content. Miso can be bought in plastic pouches at Oriental food stores and health-food stores, and used in soups, sauces, and salad dressings. Finely shredded *nori,* the silvery black dried seaweed used to wrap sushi, or *wakame,* curly shreds of dried seaweed, would be a delicious addition to this soup.

- 4 ounces firm tofu
- 4 cups High-Potassium Vegetable Stock (page 143)
- 1½ tablespoons miso, preferably barley or brown rice
- ½ cup thinly sliced scallions
- 1 tablespoon finely shredded *nori* (optional)

Cut the tofu into 12 cubes. Set aside. Bring the stock to a boil in a medium saucepan over high heat. Reduce the heat, add the tofu, and simmer for 5 minutes.

In a cup, combine the miso and ¼ cup of the hot stock and mix until smooth. Stir the miso mixture into the stock-tofu mixture, heat just until the soup reaches a boil, then serve immediately in heated bowls, garnished with the scallions and, if desired, *nori* shreds.

Serves 4

MARCO POLO CHICKEN AND PASTA SALAD

278
CALORIES PER SERVING

Julienne strips of carrots, snow peas, bell peppers, zucchini, shiitake mushrooms, and chicken make a vivid textural and color contrast with the brown soba noodles. The spicy fresh ginger dressing can be made ahead.

4 ounces boneless, skinless chicken breast
3 ounces buckwheat soba noodles (available at Oriental food stores)
2 carrots, cut into fine julienne
2 ounces snow pea pods, trimmed and cut into julienne
2 ounces fresh shiitake mushrooms, ends trimmed and cut into fine julienne
1 small red bell pepper, cut into fine julienne
1 small yellow bell pepper, cut into fine julienne
1 small zucchini, cut into fine julienne
½ cup sliced water chestnuts

GINGER DRESSING
2 tablespoons Szechuan peppercorns, or to taste, or 3 or 4 drops hot pepper sauce
1 tablespoon Oriental sesame oil
2 tablespoons safflower oil
2 tablespoons rice wine vinegar
¼ cup low-sodium soy sauce
½ cup Low-Sodium Chicken Stock (page 141)
2 tablespoons grated fresh ginger
1 tablespoon minced shallots or garlic
2 tablespoons chopped Italian parsley
Vegetable seasoning
Freshly ground white pepper
Sesame seeds

Place the chicken breast in a medium saucepan, add water to cover, and bring to a simmer over high heat. Reduce the heat, cover the pan, and poach the chicken for 12 to 15 minutes, or until cooked. Drain and let cool. Cut into julienne and place in a large bowl.

Meanwhile, bring 2 to 3 quarts of water to a boil in a saucepan. Add the noodles and cook until al dente, 3 to 7 minutes. Drain the noodles and cool them under cold running water. Drain again and add to the mixing bowl with the chicken.

Next, cook the vegetables. Bring a deep pot of water to a boil. Place the carrots in a strainer and submerge them in the boiling water. Blanch the carrots for 1 minute or less, lift the strainer out of the pan, and transfer the carrots to a bowl of cold water. Blanch the snow peas for 20 seconds and the mushrooms for 40 seconds, transferring each vegetable to the bowl of cold water after it has cooked.

Drain the vegetables, add to the mixing bowl, along with the bell peppers, zucchini, and water chestnuts, and toss gently.

To make the dressing, place the peppercorns, with their hulls, in a small skillet over medium heat, and cook 1 to 2 minutes, or until aromatic, shaking the pan 4 or 5 times. Transfer the peppercorns to a mortar and crush them into a powder. Shake the powder through a fine sieve and discard the hulls. Transfer the pepper powder to a small mixing bowl. Add the oils, vinegar, soy sauce, stock, ginger, shallots, parsley, and vegetable seasoning and white pepper to taste. Whisk the dressing until well mixed and pour it over the chicken salad. Toss again until all the salad ingredients are coated with dressing. Cover the bowl with plastic wrap, and refrigerate for several hours to let the flavors blend.

Serve the salad in shallow soup bowls, sprinkled with sesame seeds.

Serves 4

COLD SLICED ORANGES IN GRAND MARNIER SAUCE

170
CALORIES PER SERVING

This cooling dessert, an adaptation of an Italian recipe for oranges marinated in orange and lemon juices, tastes best if made the night before. Doubled or tripled, this is a welcome dessert for a dinner party.

4 large navel oranges
1½ cups fresh orange juice
2 tablespoons Grand Marnier
¼ cup fructose

Grate the zest from 2 of the oranges and reserve. With a citrus zester, remove the zest from 1 orange and reserve the strips separately. Holding the fruit over a bowl to catch the juice, peel all the oranges, cutting away the white pith. Cut each orange into 5 or 6 slices, then cut the slices in half and reserve.

In a saucepan, bring the orange juice to a boil over high heat, add the Grand Marnier, and boil the mixture, uncovered, until it is reduced by about half, for 5 minutes. Add the fructose and continue cooking the sauce until it is syrupy, 3 to 4 minutes longer. Stir in the grated zest and let the sauce cool.

Dip the half slices of orange in the sauce and arrange them on serving plates. Divide any remaining sauce among the plates, and decorate with the reserved strips of orange zest. Cover the plates with plastic wrap and chill the desserts for at least 2 hours to blend the flavors.

Serves 4

DAY 5

DINNER

670
CALORIES

•

BAKED MARINATED ARTICHOKE HEARTS

•

BAJA GRILLED TUNA WITH SALSA PIQUANTE

•

SWEET DELICATA SQUASH

•

BROCCOLI AND CAULIFLOWER
WITH TOASTED ALMONDS

•

STRAWBERRY BUTTERMILK SHERBET

BAKED MARINATED ARTICHOKE HEARTS

245
CALORIES PER SERVING

Artichoke hearts add an indulgent touch to any meal. Keep a package of frozen artichokes in your freezer for salads, pastas, and so on.

20 cooked artichoke hearts, fresh or frozen
¾ to 1 cup Spa Vinaigrette (page 140)
¾ cup Herbed Whole Wheat Bread Crumbs (page 140)
¾ cup freshly grated Parmesan cheese

If using frozen artichoke hearts, thaw and drain them. Pat the artichoke hearts dry and place them in a baking dish just large enough to hold them in a single layer. Pour the vinaigrette over them and let the mixture marinate for at least 1 hour.

Preheat the oven to 350° F.

Sprinkle the artichoke hearts with the bread crumbs and then the grated cheese. Bake for 8 to 10 minutes, or until the tops are golden brown. Serve immediately.

Serves 4

VARIATION: ARTICHOKE HEARTS STUFFED WITH CRABMEAT

73
CALORIES EACH

Instead of marinating the artichokes, stuff the hearts with 1 cup of fresh crabmeat, combined with 2 tablespoons each of green and red bell pepper, 1 tablespoon chopped chives, 1 tablespoon fresh lemon juice, and ½ cup nonfat plain yogurt. Bake just until warm and serve sprinkled with more chives.

BAJA GRILLED TUNA

165
CALORIES PER SERVING

Fresh tuna is now available much of the year. Swordfish steaks, however, are delicious too.

4 4-ounce yellowfin tuna steaks
1 tablespoon minced shallots
1½ teaspoons minced garlic
½ cup fresh lime juice

Place the tuna steaks in a shallow nonreactive dish. Combine the shallots, garlic, and lime juice in a cup, pour over the tuna, and cover with plastic wrap. Refrigerate and let the fish marinate for 1 to 2 hours.

Preheat a grill or the broiler.

Grill the steaks for 2½ to 3 minutes on each side, or until the fish is seared on the outside but still pink inside. While the fish is cooking, warm the salsa over moderate heat.

To serve, place a tuna steak on each warmed serving plate and spoon one-quarter of the salsa over it. Arrange the squash and the broccoli and cauliflower on the plate and serve at once.

Serves 4

SALSA PIQUANTE

50
CALORIES PER SERVING

This lively condiment adds a tangy zip to egg, fish, and chicken dishes for a very modest addition of calories. Increase the amount of chile if you like it *really* hot.

4 medium tomatoes
1 large yellow bell pepper
1 to 2 tablespoons minced jalapeño peppers
1 cup chopped scallions (including greens)
½ cup chopped fresh coriander or parsley
½ cup fresh lime juice

Peel and seed the tomatoes and cut them into ¼-inch dice. Core and seed the bell pepper and cut into ¼-inch dice. Place the tomatoes in a nonreactive bowl and add the jalapeño peppers, scallions, cilantro, lime juice, and diced bell pepper. Mix well and cover with plastic wrap. Leave at room temperature while the tuna marinates.

Makes 3 cups

SWEET DELICATA SQUASH

80
CALORIES PER SERVING

Delicata squash has a lovely yellow skin with green stripes. In season during the fall and winter, it's naturally sweet, but much lower in calories than acorn squash. For this recipe, we've cut the squash into chunks and steamed it in its skin, but it's just as easy to cut off the skin with a vegetable peeler before cooking. If you have only 1 steamer, keep the squash warm in a preheated 200° F. oven while you cook the broccoli and cauliflower.

1 large delicata squash (about 1½ to 2 pounds)

Rinse the squash and cut into triangular pieces. Place the pieces in a steamer over boiling water and steam for 12 to 15 minutes, or until tender when pierced with a fork. Transfer the squash to a plate, cover with foil, and keep warm until serving time.

Serves 4

BROCCOLI AND CAULIFLOWER WITH TOASTED ALMONDS

75
CALORIES PER SERVING

A handsome green-and-white combination. The natural (another term for unblanched) almonds add crunch, so you might want to cook the vegetables about a minute longer than usual.

2 cups cauliflower florets
2 cups broccoli florets
¼ cup sliced natural almonds

Place the cauliflower in a steamer basket, place over boiling water, and steam for 3 minutes. Add the broccoli to the steamer and cook about 5 minutes longer, or until both vegetables are almost fork-tender.

Meanwhile, put the almonds in a small skillet, place over moderate heat, and toast them for 2 to 3 minutes, or until they are golden brown, shaking the pan almost constantly to keep them from burning.

Transfer the vegetables to the serving plate and sprinkle with almonds.

Serves 4

STRAWBERRY BUTTERMILK SHERBET

55
CALORIES PER SERVING

Buttermilk lends character to this blush-pink sherbet. For under 15 calories more, puree an extra cup of strawberries and reserve to use as sauce.

1½ cups fresh or unsweetened frozen strawberries
2 cups buttermilk
¼ cup fresh lemon juice
¼ cup fructose

Puree the strawberries in a food processor fitted with the steel blade. Add the buttermilk, lemon juice, and fructose and process briefly. Chill the mixture, then freeze in an electric or hand-cranked ice-cream maker, following the manufacturer's instructions.

To make the sherbet in your freezer, transfer the mixture to a bowl and place in the freezer. When the liquid has frozen solid, about 2 to 3 hours, remove it from the freezer and, with a fork, break it into large chunks. Place the chunks in a food processor and process with the steel blade until smooth and creamy. Return to the bowl and freeze for at least 30 minutes more.

Makes 1 quart, serving 6 to 8

CUBANO BLACK BEAN SOUP

•

APPLE-PUMPKIN SOUP

•

ESCAROLE SOUP

•

THREE GREENS SOUP

•

CHILLED PEACH ALMOND SOUP

•

ESCAROLE SOUP

190
CALORIES PER SERVING

A vitamin-rich soup with a surprisingly delicate, almost summery flavor. If you don't have leftover cooked brown rice, add 3 tablespoons of raw orzo (rice-shaped pasta) 15 minutes before the end of cooking.

- 1 large head escarole
- 2 leeks (white part only)
- 1 cup canned low-sodium tomatoes, drained
- 2 tablespoons extra-virgin olive oil
- 1 teaspoon minced garlic
- 6 cups Low-Sodium Chicken Stock (page 141)
- ½ cup cooked brown rice
- 1 tablespoon chopped fresh basil
  Vegetable seasoning
  Freshly ground black pepper
- ¼ cup freshly grated Parmesan cheese

Trim off the bottom of the head of escarole and separate the leaves. Wash them well in several changes of water, then drain and shred the leaves. Trim the leeks, wash them thoroughly, and slice. Chop the tomatoes.

Heat the oil in a large heavy saucepan over moderate heat. Add the leeks and garlic and sauté 5 to 6 minutes, or until the leeks are barely golden; do not let them brown. Add the escarole and tomatoes and sauté 7 to 8 minutes, or until the escarole is soft.

Add the stock, raise the heat, and bring the soup to a boil. Reduce the heat, cover the kettle, and simmer the soup for 20 minutes. Add the rice and basil and simmer 15 minutes longer. Add vegetable seasoning and pepper to taste and ladle the soup into heated soup plates. Pass the grated cheese separately.

Serves 4

THREE GREENS SOUP

288
CALORIES PER SERVING

Swiss chard, spinach, and sorrel are combined in this ravishing jade-green spring soup, which provides over 100 percent of the daily requirement for vitamins A and C and more than one-third of the daily calcium requirement.

- 1 quart Low-Sodium Chicken Stock (page 141)
- 12 ounces Swiss chard, with ribs
- 8 ounces fresh sorrel leaves, well washed
- 3 ounces spinach, well washed and tough stems removed
- 3 fresh tarragon sprigs
- ¼ cup safflower oil
- 1 medium onion, chopped
- 2 teaspoons minced garlic
- 6 scallions, finely sliced
- 1½ to 2 tablespoons whole wheat flour
- 1 to 1½ cups evaporated skim milk
  Vegetable seasoning
  Freshly ground black pepper

In a 2½- to 3-quart saucepan, bring the stock to a boil over high heat.

Wash the chard well and cut out the ribs. Cut the ribs into 1-inch pieces and add to the boiling stock. Reduce the heat and simmer the chard ribs for 5 minutes. Add the chard leaves, sorrel, spinach, and tarragon to the stock and continue to simmer.

Meanwhile, heat the oil in a small skillet over moderate heat. Add the onion, garlic, and scallions and sauté for 4 to 5 minutes, or until the onion is translucent. Stir in the flour and cook, stirring constantly, for 4 to 5 minutes, or until the flour is cooked but not browned.

Gradually add the roux to the soup, stirring until the liquid is somewhat thickened. Continue to simmer the soup, uncovered, for 30 minutes. Transfer the mixture to a blender or food processor fitted with the steel blade and puree.

Return the soup to the saucepan and bring to a boil over moderate heat. Add the milk and season to taste with vegetable seasoning and pepper. Serve in heated soup bowls.

Serves 4

CHILLED PEACH ALMOND SOUP

173
CALORIES PER SERVING

Perfectly ripe fresh peaches, pureed with citrus juices and yogurt and flavored with almond extract, make a beautiful, warmly colored pastel soup. If you'd like to serve this soup out of season, use enough unsweetened frozen sliced peaches to make 2 cups of puree, and don't forget to add the lemon juice.

- 2 pounds ripe peaches
- 2 tablespoons fresh lemon juice
- 1 cup fresh orange juice
- 1 cup nonfat plain yogurt
- 1 tablespoon honey, or to taste
- 2 tablespoons almond extract

Bring a large pot of water to a boil and add the peaches. Blanch the fruit for 10 to 15 seconds, just long enough to loosen the skins. Transfer the peaches to a bowl of cold water. Put the lemon juice in another bowl. When the peaches are cool enough to handle, slip off their skins, cut them in half, and remove the pits. Toss each pitted peach half in the lemon juice as you go.

Transfer the peaches to a food processor and puree the fruit. Add the orange juice, yogurt, honey, and almond extract and process briefly. Refrigerate the soup and serve in chilled bowls.

Serves 4

MORE SPA

DESSERTS

CHILLED LIME SOUFFLÉ

132
CALORIES PER SERVING

Light and luscious, this pale green lime soufflé rises majestically over the rim of its dish, the perfect dessert for a special summer meal. In this recipe, egg whites, egg yolks, and skim milk are all beaten separately and at different temperatures. It will be easiest to make the soufflé if you have at least 2 stainless-steel mixing bowls and both a hand-held and a stationary electric mixer.

¼ cup skim milk
⅔ cup nonfat dry milk
¾ cup plus 2 teaspoons fructose
4 large eggs
2 egg whites
2 teaspoons unflavored gelatin
¼ cup cold water
1 teaspoon vanilla extract
Grated zest of 1 lime
Juice of 5 limes
Lime zest julienne for garnish

Pour the skim milk and nonfat dry milk into a medium mixing bowl, preferably stainless steel, and place the bowl with the beaters of an electric mixer in the freezer. Chill until the milk becomes slushy, 30 to 45 minutes.

Meanwhile, cut a piece of foil long enough to wrap around the top of a 1½-quart soufflé dish with 2 inches of overlap. Fold the foil in half lengthwise, wrap it around the dish, leaving 3 inches extending above the top of the dish, and tape the overlap. Spray the inside of the dish and foil collar with vegetable cooking spray and sprinkle with fructose, shaking out any excess. (If you prefer, make foil collars for eight 3-ounce soufflé cups, then spray them with vegetable cooking spray and sprinkle with fructose.)

Separate the eggs, placing the yolks in a large stainless-steel mixing bowl and the whites in another large (but not necessarily stainless-steel)

bowl. Leave the whites at room temperature while you prepare the yolks.

Add ½ cup of fructose to the yolks and stir just until mixed. Place 1 inch of water in a saucepan large enough to support the bowl containing the egg yolks as if it were the top of a double boiler. The bottom of the mixing bowl should not touch the water. Place the saucepan over moderate heat and heat the water until it is quite hot but not simmering. Reduce the heat to low, place the bowl of egg yolks over the pan, and heat the eggs, stirring with a spoon, until they are warm. Beat the eggs with a hand-held electric mixer at high speed until they are light, lemon-colored, and tripled in volume, 5 to 8 minutes. Check the water in the saucepan occasionally to see that it does not come near a simmer. Remove the egg yolk mixture from the saucepan and set aside.

In a cup, sprinkle the gelatin over the cold water and let soften 5 minutes. Place the cup in a shallow saucepan of very hot water and stir just until the gelatin is dissolved. Let the gelatin mixture cook, but do not let it set.

Remove the skim milk mixture and beaters from the freezer. Add the 2 teaspoons of fructose and the vanilla and beat at low speed for a few moments. Beat in the cooled gelatin and beat the mixture at high speed until soft peaks form. Store the whipped milk mixture in the refrigerator while you beat the egg whites.

Add the remaining ¼ cup of fructose to the egg whites and, with clean beaters, beat at high speed until stiff but not dry.

Fold the lime zest and juice into the egg yolk mixture. Stir in about one-quarter of the beaten whites, then fold in the remaining whites. Fold in the whipped milk mixture.

Spoon the soufflé into the prepared dish, smoothing the top with a spatula, and chill until firm. Remove the foil collar before serving, and garnish with lime zest julienne.

Serves 8

APPLESAUCE SPICE CAKE

189
CALORIES PER SERVING

A delicious variation on gingerbread, this homey cake is made even moister by the addition of applesauce. Leftover cake can be refrigerated or frozen for quite a while.

¼ cup safflower oil
½ cup molasses
½ cup honey
2 cups whole wheat flour
1¼ teaspoons baking soda
1 teaspoon ground cinnamon
¼ teaspoon ground cloves
¼ teaspoon ground ginger
¼ teaspoon freshly grated nutmeg
1 cup unsweetened applesauce
1 medium apple, peeled, cored, and coarsely chopped
1 large egg, beaten
½ cup raisins
¼ cup wheat germ

Preheat the oven to 350° F. Spray a 9-inch-square baking pan with vegetable cooking spray.

Place the oil, molasses, and honey in a small saucepan, place over moderate heat, and cook until very hot. Set aside until cool.

Sift the flour, baking soda, cinnamon, cloves, ginger, and nutmeg into a mixing bowl, then add the oil mixture, applesauce, apple, egg, raisins, and wheat germ. Stir to combine well.

Turn the batter into the pan and bake for 25 to 30 minutes, or until a cake tester or toothpick inserted in the center comes out clean. Let the cake cool in the pan on a rack. Cut into 16 pieces.

Serves 16

APPLE-CRANBERRY PIE WITH LATTICE CRUST

247
CALORIES PER SERVING

Serve this charming country pie at a fall or winter holiday meal. The crunchy honey-oatmeal crust, easily mixed by hand and pressed into the pie plate, is similar to a graham cracker crust, but a little stickier. In summertime, substitute a quart of blueberries for the cranberries and apples.

OATMEAL CRUST
- 2 egg whites
- ¾ cup honey
- ½ cup skim milk
- 3½ to 4 cups old-fashioned rolled oats
- ⅔ cup whole wheat pastry flour

CREAM CHEESE FILLING
- 5 teaspoons fructose
- 8 ounces low-fat cream cheese, softened to room temperature
- 2 teaspoons fresh lemon juice

CRANBERRY-APPLE TOPPING
- 1 teaspoon ground cinnamon
- ½ teaspoon ground allspice
- ¼ teaspoon ground mace
- ¾ cup fructose
- 1 tablespoon cornstarch
- 3 tablespoons water
- Grated zest and juice of 1 lemon
- 2 cups raw fresh or frozen cranberries
- 4 medium tart apples (preferably Granny Smith), peeled, cored, and coarsely chopped

To prepare the crust, in a small mixing bowl, whisk the egg whites until frothy. Stir in the honey and milk and blend well. In a larger bowl, combine 3½ cups of the oats and the flour and toss with your hands to mix well. Pour in the egg white mixture, stirring with a fork until all the ingredients are evenly mixed. If the crust seems a little moist, stir in additional rolled oats

1 tablespoon at a time. If it seems too dry, stir in water 1 teaspoon at a time.

Spray a 10-inch pie plate with vegetable cooking spray and pat two-thirds of the crust mixture into the bottom and up the sides of the plate. The crust will be ⅛ to ¼ inch thick. Cover the crust with foil or plastic wrap and refrigerate until firm, 30 to 45 minutes. Wrap the remaining crust mixture in foil and refrigerate.

To prepare the filling, pulverize the fructose with a mortar and pestle; you should have 5 to 6 tablespoons. Place the cream cheese in a mixing bowl and cream it with an electric mixer until light and fluffy. Add the fructose and lemon juice and beat until well mixed.

Remove the chilled piecrust from the refrigerator and spread the filling over it evenly. Cover the pie again and chill it while you make the topping.

Preheat the oven to 350° F.

Combine the cinnamon, allspice, mace, fructose, and cornstarch in a small bowl. In a medium saucepan over high heat, bring the water and lemon zest and juice to a boil. Add the cranberries and return to a boil over high heat. Cook, uncovered, until the berries begin to pop, about 5 to 7 minutes. Remove the cranberry mixture from the heat, stir in the apples and the cinnamon mixture, and stir until well mixed. Spread the topping evenly over the cream cheese filling.

Remove the remaining oatmeal crust mixture from the refrigerator. Break off pieces of the mixture, place them on a flat surface, and, with your hands, roll them into strips about ⅜ inch in diameter. Arrange the strips over the topping in a lattice pattern, draping the strips over each other at the intersections. (There is no need to join the strips where they meet, because the crust will settle into one level as it bakes.)

Bake the pie for 25 to 30 minutes, or until the crust is nicely browned and set. Let cool and then chill the pie before serving.

Serves 16

FILO TULIPES WITH VANILLA ICE CREAM

150
CALORIES PER SERVING

This may well become your favorite dessert for entertaining—delicately browned, flaky filo tulipes cradling scoops of rich vanilla ice cream. The tulipes are far simpler to make than their appearance would lead you to believe. You can prepare the ice cream in advance, then assemble the dessert just before serving. Decorate the tulipes with fresh berries or sliced peaches, if you like.

- 2 14 x 18-inch sheets filo dough
- ½ recipe Vanilla Ice Cream (page 145)

Preheat the oven to 375° F. Spray four 1-cup soufflé dishes or custard cups with vegetable cooking spray.

With a sharp knife, trim off and discard 4 inches from the top of each filo sheet, leaving two 14-inch squares. Cut each sheet into four 7-inch squares, and stack all the squares so the dough does not dry out.

Spray the top sheet with vegetable cooking spray and place it on the counter. Spray the second sheet with vegetable cooking spray and place it catercornered on top of the first sheet, to form an 8-pointed star. Lift both sheets off the counter and press them into a soufflé dish. Make 3 more tulipes with the remaining filo.

Place the dishes on a baking sheet and bake for 8 to 10 minutes, or until golden. Remove the tulipes carefully from the dishes (they are quite brittle) and let cool on racks. Store for 2 or 3 days in airtight containers at room temperature.

To serve, arrange the tulipes on 4 dessert plates and place two ¼-cup scoops of ice cream in each.

Serves 4

special

occasions

For people who think that special occasions are synonymous with overindulgence, New Spa Food will come as a pleasant surprise indeed. Our special occasion menus and recipes have been devised to satisfy much more than hunger alone; they also appease those insidious cravings that are invariably aroused whenever a party and food are mentioned in the same breath. Because we've packed so much flavor and variety into these menus, your guests will be astounded to learn they don't even have to feel guilty for indulging themselves.

In keeping with our "real life" Spa philosophy, we give guests at the Spa the opportunity to make the same kinds of menu choices they'll have to make when they return home. By the same token, in the menus that follow you and your family and friends will have the ability to choose from among the dishes offered at each meal, to decide how much of each they want to eat, whether to have a bite of *both* desserts if two are offered (or none at all), and whether to partake of any wine or other alcoholic beverages that are offered. That's why we don't give a total calorie count for these menus, but rather the individual calories-per-serving count for each recipe. Bear in mind, however, that at a buffet or picnic you are more likely to eat considerably less than a full serving of each dish when there are many to choose from.

In this section, we present eight menus for occasions as various as a summer clambake, a winter tea, a tailgate picnic, an open house, a fall harvest buffet, an après-ski supper, a brunch, and a formal dinner. But you don't need a special menu to incorporate New Spa Food into your celebrations; many of the recipes in the previous two sections of this book can be mixed and matched to make your own festive menus.

For instance, we think our miniature pizzas would be a great hit at a party for children *and* their parents. Whip up several batches of the dough in the food processor and, while it's rising, prepare as many of the special toppings on page 51 as you like. To make a basic pizza topping, cut thin slices of plum tomatoes and low-fat mozzarella and layer them with basil leaves and drops of olive oil on the rounds of partially baked crust. Let each guest add his or her individual topping selections before the final baking, then watch the pizzas disappear hot from the oven.

For a New Year's Day at home, make one or two of our hearty Spa soups (see pages 98 to 99) and serve them with platters of pita pocket sandwiches filled with smoked chicken breast (page 114) or slices of roast pork tenderloin (page 70) and any of our crisp, leafy Spa salads. Cold marinated orange sections (page 91) are a refreshing finale.

Pamper the one you love with an intimate dinner for two—even nicer for you both if it can be prepared largely in advance. In warm weather, a chilled soup and a salad are superlative choices. Try the Broccoli and Basil Soup (page 58), and serve the Marco Polo Chicken and Pasta Salad (page 91) as the main course. For a nice summer flourish, add the fresh Blueberry Ice Cream (page 47) for dessert.

As you can see, it's not heavy sauces, sugary sweets, or salty snack foods that make an occasion special. And, conversely, there is no reason that a guilty conscience and a leaden stomach need result from a celebratory meal.

Once you've been converted to the New Spa Food way of cooking, you'll find lots of occasions to introduce friends and family to the pleasures of healthier eating. The office workers' pot-luck lunch—a citified version of the old-fashioned church supper—is a new tradition in the making. Everyone brings a different portable dish of New Spa Food to share with the group. Cold soups, sandwiches, nonwilting salads, fruits, and cookies are the way to go. Be sure to use real cutlery and napkins if you can.

Or consider making yourself an extravagant bagged lunch to eat at your desk or, better yet, on a park bench beside a fountain. You can pack a bag with leftover white bean salad, sliced tomatoes and onions, and grilled leg of lamb from our Open House menu, or a vacuum flask of any of the Spa soups and a hearty muffin.

You'll be proud to share the recipes in this book and your own New Spa Food with your family and friends. Any meal can be festive if you plan it that way. Beautifully presented food tastes better, so it's always worth taking a little extra time to make each dish look appealing. But the most important ingredient is your own convivial spirit, the pleasure you take in sharing good food with others, because good food does more than nourish the body and soul: it fosters good fellowship among those who partake of it.

B R U N C H

WHITE SANGRIA

•

CHILLED CANTALOUPE SOUP
WITH MIXED PEPPERCORNS

•

CORNMEAL CRÊPES WITH
HOT AND SPICY SHRIMP

•

SHREDDED CUCUMBER SALAD
WITH RASPBERRY VINEGAR AND
CHIVE DRESSING

•

LEMON WAFERS

•

WHITE SANGRIA

110

CALORIES PER SERVING

Luscious summer fruits add color and fragrance to this refreshing sangria. For this recipe, we use equal amounts of dry white wine and mineral water, but you can add another cup or so of mineral water without diluting the flavor too much for a lighter sangria spritzer.

1 peach
1 nectarine
1 or 2 apricots
½ cup **Queen Anne cherries**
1½ cups **dry white wine**
1½ cups **sparkling mineral water**
   or seltzer
Ice cubes

Wash all the fruit. Cut the peach, nectarine, and apricot into wedges and discard the pits. Place the wedges and cherries in a large pitcher, add the wine and mineral water, and stir to blend. Stir in ice cubes and serve.

Serves 4

CHILLED CANTALOUPE SOUP WITH MIXED PEPPERCORNS

106

CALORIES PER SERVING

Fresh-tasting and not too sweet, this chilled cantaloupe soup is packed with vitamins A and C. The mild cantaloupe flavor is heightened by melon liqueur, and the balsamic vinegar and cracked peppercorns provide a little zip.

2 cups **fresh orange juice**
¼ cup **melon liqueur**
1 large **cantaloupe**
1 tablespoon **balsamic vinegar**
1 tablespoon **grated lemon zest**
1 teaspoon **mixed cracked white,**
   black, and red peppercorns

Pour the orange juice and liqueur into a 1-quart saucepan and bring to a boil over high heat. Cook, uncovered, until reduced by half, 5 to 7 minutes. Let cool.

Peel the cantaloupe, cut it in half, and scoop out the seeds. Cut the fruit into chunks and puree in a food processor fitted with the steel blade. You should have about 3 cups of puree.

Transfer the cantaloupe to a bowl, stir in the orange juice mixture, vinegar, lemon zest, and peppercorns, and chill.

Serves 4 to 6

CORNMEAL CRÊPES WITH HOT AND SPICY SHRIMP

326

CALORIES PER SERVING

Crunchy cornmeal crêpes can be made the night before serving and stored, covered in foil, in the refrigerator. Reheat the crêpes, still in their wrapping, for 15 to 20 minutes in a preheated 350° F. oven before filling them.

CORNMEAL CRÊPES
⅓ cup **yellow cornmeal**
¾ cup **boiling water**
1 large **egg**
½ cup **skim milk, plus an additional**
   2 tablespoons if needed
1 tablespoon **safflower oil**
½ cup **whole wheat pastry flour**
¼ teaspoon **sea salt**

FILLING
1½ pounds **medium shrimp**
1½ tablespoons **extra-virgin olive oil**
¼ teaspoon **Spanish paprika**
1 teaspoon **minced garlic**
1 teaspoon **minced shallots**
1 **jalapeño pepper, seeded and sliced**
2 **tomatoes, peeled, and chopped**
1 **6½-ounce can low-sodium**
   tomato juice cocktail
¼ cup **white wine vinegar**
   Dash of hot pepper sauce
½ cup **fresh corn kernels**
3 tablespoons **chopped fresh coriander**
   Spicy vegetable seasoning
   Chive blossoms for garnish (optional)

To make the crêpe batter, place the cornmeal in a mixing bowl and stir in the boiling water. Mix well and let the cornmeal stand while you prepare the remaining ingredients.

In another bowl, beat the egg, ½ cup of the milk, and the oil. Add the flour and salt and stir until just blended. Beat in the cornmeal mixture, beating until smooth. Let the batter stand 15 to 20 minutes.

To make the filling, shell and devein the shrimp. Heat the oil in a heavy skillet over moderately high heat, add the shrimp and paprika, and sear the shrimp on both sides. Using a slotted spoon, transfer the shrimp to a warm platter and reserve.

Add the garlic, shallots, and jalapeño pepper to the skillet and sauté the mixture over moderate heat for about 2 minutes. Add the tomatoes, tomato juice cocktail, vinegar, and hot pepper sauce and cook over high heat until the mixture is reduced by one-quarter, about 5 minutes. Add the corn and cook 2 to 3 minutes more, until the corn is barely cooked. (The sauce can be made in advance to this point.) Add the shrimp, and cook until they are heated through. Stir in the coriander and spicy vegetable seasoning to taste.

To make the crêpes, spray an 8-inch nonstick crêpe pan with vegetable cooking spray and heat the pan over high heat. Stir the batter; it should be the consistency of heavy cream. Add the remaining milk, a teaspoon at a time, to adjust the consistency, if necessary. Ladle 3 tablespoons of the batter into the skillet, swirl the pan so that the batter covers the bottom in a thin layer, and cook the crêpe about 30 seconds, or until the top looks dry and the bottom is golden brown. Turn the crêpe with a spatula and brown the other side, about 5 seconds. Continue making crêpes, stirring the batter before making each one and stacking them as they are finished. If using immediately, cover them with a towel to keep warm. You will have about 8 to 10 crêpes. Leftover crêpes can be stored, well wrapped in foil, in the freezer for up to 1 month.

To serve, place 2 crêpes on each of 4 heated plates. (Alternatively, the crêpes can be made and served on a platter.) Spoon 2 to 3 tablespoons of the shrimp mixture over half of each crêpe, garnish with chive blossoms, if desired, and fold over the other half of the crêpe.

Serves 4

SHREDDED CUCUMBER SALAD WITH RASPBERRY VINEGAR AND CHIVE DRESSING

62
CALORIES PER SERVING

Less is more in this cool cucumber salad. Raspberry vinegar, in a barely-there vinaigrette, intensifies the fresh taste of the grated vegetable.

1 large European cucumber (about 1 pound)

DRESSING
1½ tablespoons raspberry vinegar
1½ tablespoons walnut oil
2 tablespoons sparkling mineral water
3 grinds white pepper
3 tablespoons snipped fresh chives or dill

Wash the cucumber and trim off the ends, but do not peel it. Grate the cucumber in a food processor fitted with the fine shredder or put it through the fine shredding blade of a hand-powered vegetable cutter. If neither piece of equipment is available, use a regular, medium-blade shredder. Transfer the cucumber to a mixing bowl.

Place all the dressing ingredients in a small bowl and whisk until combined.

Pour the dressing over the cucumber and toss the salad lightly with your hands. Serve the salad as soon as possible, while it is still crisp.

Serves 4

LEMON WAFERS

51
CALORIES PER COOKIE

A good year-round cookie that is as tasty with a fruit sorbet as it is with hot spiced cider, these are meltingly delicious. It's best to make them on a sunny, dry day, because too much humidity turns them limp. At the Spa we pipe the batter from a pastry bag, but for the home cook, a teaspoon will do quite well. Store the cookies in an airtight container at room temperature.

10 tablespoons (1¼ sticks) corn oil margarine, softened
1 cup fructose
½ cup honey
2 large eggs
2 egg whites
1 teaspoon vanilla extract
1 tablespoon lemon extract
Grated zest of 2 large lemons
2¼ cups sifted whole wheat pastry flour

Preheat the oven to 350° F. Line baking sheets with parchment paper.

In a mixing bowl, with an electric mixer or by hand, cream the margarine, fructose, and honey until the mixture is light and fluffy. Beat in the eggs and egg whites one at a time. Beat in the vanilla, lemon extract, and lemon zest. Fold in the flour, taking care not to overmix the batter.

Drop teaspoonfuls of the batter 2 inches apart on the baking sheets. Bake for 7 to 8 minutes, or until golden brown around the edges. Let the cookies cool on the parchment paper, either on the baking sheets or on a counter.

Makes 60 to 72 cookies

TAILGATE

PICNIC

HIGH-POTASSIUM
COUNTRY VEGETABLE
SOUP
(page 143)
•
SMOKED CHICKEN BREAST
SANDWICHES
•
GREEN BEANS AND
CAULIFLOWER VINAIGRETTE
WITH
CONFETTI VEGETABLES
•
ZESTY POTATO SALAD
•
BEET SALAD
•
APRICOT CRUNCH BARS
•
HOT CRANBERRY-APPLE-
CINNAMON TODDY
•

SMOKED CHICKEN BREAST SANDWICHES

350
CALORIES PER SERVING

Smoke-cured chicken breasts are a versatile addition to the shelves of delicatessens and better butchers. They have a mild smoky flavor that never overwhelms the delicious taste of chicken. Use the breasts (smoked turkey breasts are also available) as we do here in a sandwich, or for salads (see Cos Cob Salad, page 118). Always remove the tough, fatty skin from the breast before serving.

½ cup Dijon mustard
1 tablespoon rice wine vinegar
1 to 1½ tablespoons green peppercorns, drained
2 boneless smoked chicken breasts (about 10 ounces each)
1 medium avocado
2 whole wheat pita breads
1 cup mixed crunchy sprouts (lentil, adzuki, sweet pea, alfalfa, or radish sprouts)

In a cup, combine the mustard, vinegar, and peppercorns and let stand while you prepare the chicken and avocado.

Remove and discard the skin from the chicken and scrape off any pockets of fat. Cut the breasts into slices. Peel the avocado, cut in half lengthwise, and discard the pit. Cut the avocado into quarters and slice thin.

Cut the pita pockets in half and spread some of the mustard mixture evenly inside each piece. Place one-quarter of the chicken, avocado, and sprout mixture inside each pocket.

Wrap the sandwiches carefully in plastic wrap.

Serves 4

GREEN BEANS AND CAULIFLOWER VINAIGRETTE WITH CONFETTI VEGETABLES

85
CALORIES PER SERVING

Here's a high-fiber salad with lots of flavor and crunch. The vinaigrette will turn the bright green beans a sickly olive color if added too soon, so dress the salad just before serving.

½ pound green beans
2 cups cauliflower florets
¼ cup finely diced red bell pepper
¼ cup finely diced yellow bell pepper
½ cup Spa Vinaigrette (page 140)

Trim the ends from the beans and steam them for about 4 minutes, or until crisp-tender. Immediately plunge the beans into a bowl of cold water to stop the cooking and set the color. Steam the cauliflower for 4 minutes and add to the bowl of cold water. (You can steam the vegetables together if your steamer is large enough.)

Drain the beans and cauliflower and place in a bowl. Add the bell peppers, cover the bowl, and refrigerate, if not using immediately.

Before serving, bring the vegetables to room temperature, add the vinaigrette, and toss to mix. Serve at once.

Serves 4

ZESTY POTATO SALAD

120
CALORIES PER SERVING

"Zesty" is the operative word in this noncreamy picnic salad of just-cooked potatoes marinated in wine vinegar and mustard.

¾ pound Red Bliss potatoes
2½ tablespoons red wine vinegar
1 tablespoon whole-grain mustard
Freshly ground black pepper
¼ cup sliced scallions
1½ tablespoons capers, drained
2 tablespoons snipped fresh dill
2 tablespoons chopped Italian parsley
2 tablespoons safflower oil

Place the potatoes in a medium saucepan, cover with cold water, and bring to a boil over high heat. Reduce the heat, cover the pan, and boil the potatoes until tender, about 25 minutes.

Drain the potatoes, halve them if they are large, then cut into thick slices. Place them in a mixing bowl. In a cup, combine the vinegar, mustard, and black pepper to taste. Pour the mixture over the potatoes and toss to mix well. Cover the bowl and let the potatoes stand for 30 minutes.

Add the scallions, capers, dill, and parsley and toss to mix. Pour the oil over the salad and mix gently but thoroughly. Cover the salad and refrigerate if not using at once. Bring the salad to room temperature before serving.

Serves 4

BEET SALAD

100

CALORIES PER SERVING

Freshly cooked beets (see page 74) will be tastier, but if you're pressed for time, by all means used sliced canned beets. Either way, they're a natural energy source and diuretic.

    2 cups sliced cooked beets
    ½ cup plus 1 tablespoon sliced
        scallions
    2 tablespoons red wine vinegar
    2 tablespoons rice wine vinegar
    ⅛ teaspoon freshly grated nutmeg
        Dash of ground cloves
    2 tablespoons cold-pressed
        safflower oil
    ½ cup sparkling mineral water or
        seltzer

Cut the beets into thick julienne or batons and place in a mixing bowl. Add ½ cup of the scallions. In a small bowl, combine the vinegars, nutmeg, cloves, oil, and mineral water. Pour the dressing over the vegetables and toss to mix.

Cover the bowl and let the beets macerate for at least 1 hour before serving. Serve at room temperature, with the remaining tablespoon of scallions sprinkled on top.

Serves 4

APRICOT CRUNCH BARS

115

CALORIES PER COOKIE

Toasted sunflower and sesame seeds and old-fashioned rolled oats are combined with honey and apricots in this country-kitchen recipe. Children will love making and eating these cookies, so you'll have no problem with leftovers.

    12 dried apricots
    2 tablespoons sunflower seeds
    1 tablespoon unhulled sesame seeds
    1½ cups old-fashioned rolled oats
    6 tablespoons whole wheat
        pastry flour
    2 tablespoons wheat germ
        Pinch of freshly grated nutmeg
    ¼ teaspoon ground cinnamon
    2 egg whites
    ½ cup honey
    2 tablespoons cold-pressed
        safflower oil
    1½ teaspoons vanilla extract

Preheat the oven to 350° F. Spray an 8-inch-square baking dish with vegetable cooking spray.

Place the apricots in a bowl, add boiling water to cover, and plump the fruit for about 5 minutes. Drain the apricots, dry them thoroughly between paper towels, and chop coarsely. Place the apricots in a mixing bowl and reserve.

Put the sunflower and sesame seeds in a small dry skillet and shake over moderate heat for 3 to 4 minutes to toast them. Add the seeds to the apricots, along with the oats, flour, wheat germ, nutmeg, and cinnamon, and toss to combine well.

In a small bowl, beat the egg whites with a fork until frothy. Add the honey, oil, and vanilla and mix well. Stir the egg white mixture into the dry ingredients and combine well. The mixture will be quite dry.

Press the mixture into the baking dish and bake for 20 minutes, or until set. Let cool thoroughly before cutting into 16 bars.

Makes 16 bars

HOT CRANBERRY-APPLE-CINNAMON TODDY

64

CALORIES PER SERVING

The combination of cranberries and apples is an honored New England tradition. Here fruit juices, fruit teas, and cinnamon are blended in a bracing nonalcoholic brew that's bursting with vitamin C.

    1½ cups apple juice
    1½ cups cranberry juice
    1 cranberry clove tea bag
    1 cinnamon apple spice tea bag
    1 cinnamon stick

Place the apple juice, cranberry juice, tea bags, and cinnamon stick in a 1½-quart saucepan and bring to a boil over high heat. Take the pan from the heat, cover, and let steep for 10 to 15 minutes. Remove the tea bags and cinnamon sticks and pour into a warm flask. Serve the tea in mugs.

Serves 4

special occasions • *115*

O P E N

GIARDINERA
(page 50)

•

COS COB SALAD

•

SLICED TOMATOES AND
RED ONION WITH BASIL

•

WHITE BEAN SALAD

•

EGGPLANT CAVIAR

•

GRILLED BUTTERFLIED
LEG OF LAMB

•

APPLESAUCE SPICE CAKE
(page 102)

•

STRAWBERRY ROLL

•

HERBAL ICED TEA

•

HOUSE

COS COB SALAD

110

CALORIES PER SERVING

Cooked ½-inch lengths of green beans, tender young green peas, and diced celery would all be welcome additions to this refreshing, colorful salad, sparked by a lemony yogurt dressing.

6 cups coarsely chopped romaine lettuce
1 cup coarsely chopped radicchio leaves
1 cup avocado cut into ½-inch dice
1 cup seeded tomato cut into ½-inch dice
1 cup coarsely chopped scallions
1½ cups skinless smoked chicken cut into ½-inch dice
2 hard-cooked eggs, peeled and coarsely chopped
½ cup crumbled blue cheese
2 cups nonfat plain yogurt
¼ cup fresh lemon juice
Vegetable seasoning
Freshly ground white pepper

In a very large mixing bowl, combine the romaine, radicchio, avocado, tomato, scallions, chicken, eggs, and blue cheese. In a small bowl, whisk together the yogurt, lemon juice, and vegetable seasoning and white pepper to taste. Pour the dressing over the salad and toss gently to mix. Cover and chill for at least 1 hour.

Serves 12

WHITE BEAN SALAD

75

CALORIES PER SERVING

White beans, high in fiber and rich in iron and phosphorous, are a delicious and traditional accompaniment for lamb. If you decide to make the beans from scratch, soak about ⅓ cup of dried navy beans overnight in cold water to cover, drain, and add fresh water before cooking. Never add salt or any highly acidic food, such as vinegar, to beans while they're cooking, or they'll remain hard even if you boil them for hours.

6 cups cooked white beans
¾ cup sliced button mushrooms
3 tablespoons chopped red bell pepper
3 tablespoons chopped red onion
3 tablespoons chopped Italian parsley
1½ tablespoons fresh thyme leaves
6 tablespoons extra-virgin olive oil
¾ cup red wine vinegar
¾ cup water
1 tablespoon fructose
3 garlic cloves

If you are using canned beans, place them in a sieve and rinse off the salty canning liquid under cold running water, then drain the beans.

In a mixing bowl, combine the beans, mushrooms, bell pepper, onion, parsley, and thyme. In another bowl, whisk the oil, vinegar, water, and fructose. Press the garlic through a garlic press into the mixture and whisk until blended. Pour the dressing over the bean mixture and toss to mix. Cover and chill for at least 1 hour.

Serves 12

EGGPLANT CAVIAR

88

CALORIES PER SERVING

Here is our Spa interpretation of a recipe that, in one form or another, can be found in every Mediterranean cuisine. For a subtle, smoky flavor, cook the eggplant over hot coals instead of baking it. Make the dish a day or two in advance so the vegetables and vinaigrette have a chance to blend and mellow.

2 eggplants (about 2¼ pounds)
1 or 2 garlic cloves, minced
1 large Spanish onion, chopped medium fine
1 large red bell pepper, chopped medium fine
1 large green bell pepper, chopped medium fine
Juice of 1 to 2 lemons
5 tablespoons fruity extra-virgin olive oil
Freshly ground black pepper

Preheat the oven to 375° to 400° F. Line a baking sheet with foil.

Place the eggplants on the baking sheet and bake 1½ hours, or until soft and very tender, turning once.

Let the eggplants stand until cool enough to handle. One at a time, transfer them to a bowl, cut off the stem ends, and strip away the skin, scraping the pulp into the bowl. In a food processor fitted with the steel blade, process the pulp in bursts, chopping it quite fine but leaving a few lumps here and there for texture.

Transfer the pulp to a bowl and let the eggplant cool to room temperature. Add the garlic, onion, bell peppers, lemon juice, oil, and a generous grind of black pepper. Stir well and store, tightly covered, in the refrigerator for up to 3 to 4 days.

Serves 12

GRILLED BUTTERFLIED LEG OF LAMB

161
CALORIES PER SERVING

Butterflied leg of lamb is an ideal main course for a large group. With the aid of your butcher, it's amazingly simple to prepare, and because butterflying creates an unevenly thick piece of meat, during cooking parts remain rare while others are well done, allowing your guests a choice.

  1 4- to 5-pound leg of lamb, butterflied and trimmed
  3 garlic cloves, cut into slivers
  1 cup dry red wine
  ½ cup low-sodium soy sauce
  2 tablespoons rice wine vinegar
  2 tablespoons Dijon mustard
  ¼ cup chopped fresh mint
  2 tablespoons chopped fresh rosemary
  1½ teaspoons freshly ground black pepper

Remove all visible fat from the lamb. Cut slits all over the meat and insert the garlic slivers. Place the lamb in a large plastic bag and put the bag in a bowl.

In a bowl, combine the wine, soy sauce, vinegar, mustard, mint, rosemary, and pepper. Pour the marinade into the bag with the lamb, turning to coat the meat all over. Press all the air out of the bag, seal it, and place the bowl in the refrigerator. Marinate the lamb for at least 4 hours or overnight, turning occasionally.

Remove the lamb from the refrigerator 1 hour before grilling.

Prepare a charcoal or gas grill or preheat the broiler. Drain the lamb and grill for about 15 minutes on each side, basting frequently with the marinade. Let the lamb stand for about 5 minutes, then cut into thin diagonal slices.

Serves 12

STRAWBERRY ROLL

162
CALORIES PER SERVING

Our party cake roll, shown on page 101, is made from an extra-light sponge cake batter. It's best to bake the cake on the day you plan to use it and fill it close to serving time so that the jam and berries don't soak into the cake, making it soggy. Any other ripe berries that appeal to you, along with an appropriate fruit-only jam, can be substituted for the strawberries and strawberry jam. If you like, top each serving with a dollop of One-Minute Almond Cream.

CAKE ROLL
  14 egg whites, at room temperature
  1 teaspoon fresh lemon juice
  ½ teaspoon vanilla extract
  ½ teaspoon orange extract
  ½ teaspoon grated orange zest
  ½ cup honey
  1 cup sifted whole wheat pastry flour

FILLING
  2 teaspoons fructose
  ¾ cup fruit-only strawberry jam
  1 pint strawberries, thinly sliced

  1 recipe One-Minute Almond Cream

Preheat the oven to 325° F. Line a 10 x 15-inch jelly roll pan with parchment paper.

In a large mixing bowl, beat the egg whites until frothy. Add the lemon juice and beat the whites until stiff. Sprinkle the whites with the vanilla, orange extract, and orange zest, then drizzle the honey over the top and fold in. Sprinkle the flour over the whites and fold it in gently, taking care not to overmix.

Spoon the batter into the pan, smoothing the top with a spatula. Bake the cake for about 15 minutes, or just until golden brown. The sides of the cake should not pull away from the sides of the pan.

Place the baking pan on a rack and let the cake cool for about 10 to 15 minutes. Spread out a kitchen towel on a flat surface and sprinkle with the fructose. Loosen the edges of the cake with a spatula and invert the pan over the towel. Lift off the pan and carefully remove the parchment paper by folding the far edge back and gently pulling the paper toward you. Do not lift the parchment straight up off the cake when pulling it away, or the cake will tear. Roll up the cake in the towel from a long edge and refrigerate for a few hours, or until just before serving.

Unroll the cooled cake on the towel and spread with a thin layer of jam. Arrange the strawberries over the entire surface and roll up the cake from the long side, using the towel to lift the edge. Place the cake seam side down on a serving plate or long wooden board and slice just before serving. Serve with the almond cream or flavored yogurt, if desired.

Serves 10 to 12

ONE-MINUTE ALMOND CREAM

30
CALORIES PER SERVING

Just a tablespoon or so of this quickly made cream adds a special touch to even simple desserts or fruit salads.

  6 ounces low-fat cottage cheese
  3 ounces nonfat plain yogurt
  ½ teaspoon almond extract
  ½ teaspoon vanilla extract
  1 tablespoon honey

Place the cottage cheese, yogurt, almond extract, vanilla, and honey in a blender and process until smooth. Chill before serving.

Serves 10 to 12

PRÈS-SKI SUPPER

ORANGE CLOVE TEA

•

HOT "CHOCOLATE"

•

TOMATO SOUP WITH
FRESH HERBS

•

JEAN'S CHICKEN POT PIES

•

ROMAINE, SPINACH, AND
RED CABBAGE SALAD
WITH CELERY SEED
DRESSING

•

SPA GINGERBREAD

•

ORANGE CLOVE TEA

61
CALORIES PER SERVING

For an extra kick, this spiced fruit tea can be spiked with a jigger of rum.

2 cups water
2 cups fresh orange juice
3 whole cloves
4 mandarin orange tea bags

Pour the water and orange juice into a 2-quart saucepan, add the cloves and tea bags, and bring to a boil over high heat. Remove from the heat, cover, and let steep for 15 minutes. Remove the tea bags and cloves and pour the tea into mugs.

Serves 4

HOT ''CHOCOLATE''

136
CALORIES PER SERVING

Sweet, hot, and chocolaty, our carob drink is guaranteed to take the chill off. To vary the flavor, use 1 teaspoon of grated orange zest instead of the cinnamon and add a few drops of orange extract with the vanilla.

1 quart skim milk
4½ tablespoons carob powder
1 teaspoon ground cinnamon
1½ tablespoons honey
1½ teaspoons vanilla extract

Combine the milk, carob powder, cinnamon, and honey in a medium saucepan and cook over moderately low heat until very hot but not boiling, whisking 3 or 4 times. Whisk in the vanilla and serve hot in mugs.

Serves 4

TOMATO SOUP WITH FRESH HERBS

126
CALORIES PER SERVING

Six different fresh herbs scent our fortifying tomato soup. Should you be unable to find one or two of them, the soup will still be delicious. Leftovers freeze well.

1 large onion
2 celery stalks
1 carrot, peeled
1 red bell pepper, seeded and cored
1 garlic clove, minced
3 16-ounce cans low-sodium tomatoes
2 cups Low-Sodium Chicken Stock
  (page 141)
2 tablespoons chopped fresh basil
1 tablespoon chopped fresh tarragon
½ teaspoon chopped fresh marjoram
1 teaspoon snipped fresh chives or
  scallion tops
1 teaspoon chopped fresh thyme
1 teaspoon chopped fresh oregano
Vegetable seasoning
Freshly ground black pepper
Fresh chives and tarragon sprigs
for garnish

Chop the onion, celery, carrot, and bell pepper. Spray the bottom of a soup kettle with vegetable cooking spray and place the kettle over moderate heat. Add the onion and sauté for 5 minutes, or until it is translucent. Add the celery, carrot, bell pepper, and garlic and sauté 5 minutes longer.

Add the tomatoes and stock and bring to a boil over high heat. Reduce the heat, cover, and simmer until the vegetables are tender, about 15 minutes. Transfer the mixture in batches to a food processor and puree. As the soup is pureed, pour it into a large, clean saucepan.

Stir in the basil, tarragon, marjoram, chives, thyme, and oregano. Add vegetable seasoning and black pepper to taste, place over moderate

heat, and simmer 10 minutes longer. Serve in heated soup bowls, sprinkled with the chives and a sprig of tarragon.

Serves 6–8

JEAN'S CHICKEN POT PIES

334
CALORIES PER SERVING

The filo rosettes that dress up our old-fashioned pot pies look complicated, yet they are amazingly easy to make, and their crisp texture complements the creamy chicken and vegetables. The stew tastes better if it's made a day ahead of time, so there's scarcely any work involved on the day you serve it.

2½ cups Low-Sodium Chicken Stock
  (page 141)
1 pound boneless, skinless
  chicken breasts
½ cup whole wheat flour
1 tablespoon cold-pressed
  safflower oil
¼ cup dry white wine
1 medium onion, chopped
1 garlic clove, minced
2 medium carrots, peeled and cut into
  ½-inch dice
2 medium potatoes, peeled and cut
  into ½-inch dice
2 celery stalks, cut into ½-inch dice
½ cup chopped scallions
1 tablespoon chopped fresh rosemary
1 tablespoon chopped fresh parsley
1 tablespoon cornstarch mixed with
  1 tablespoon cold water
4 sheets filo

Place the stock in a heavy saucepan and boil over high heat until reduced by one-third, about 6 to 7 minutes.

Cut the chicken into ¾-inch cubes. Dredge the chicken in the flour, shaking off the excess. Heat the oil in a heavy nonstick skillet over moderately high heat, add the chicken, and sauté for 3 minutes, stirring often and watching carefully to see that it doesn't burn.

Remove the chicken from the skillet and set aside. Add the wine, onion, and garlic to the skillet, and cook over moderate heat for 2 minutes. Add the carrots and cook 4 minutes longer. Stir in the potatoes and celery and cook 4 minutes more, stirring often. Add the scallions, rosemary, parsley, reduced stock, cornstarch mixture, and reserved chicken and cook just until the sauce is thickened, 3 to 4 minutes. (The recipe can be prepared up to 12 hours ahead to this point. Let cool, cover tightly, and refrigerate if the dish will be held longer than 2 hours.)

Forty minutes before serving, preheat the oven to 350° F.

Place the chicken mixture over moderate heat and bring it almost to a boil. Divide the mixture among four 1½- to 2-cup individual casseroles.

To make the crust, spray a sheet of filo with vegetable cooking spray. Turn the sheet over and pick it up from the center, the way you would a handkerchief you were going to tuck into your pocket. Crumple the filo into a rosette and nestle it on top of one of the casseroles. Make rosettes with the remaining filo sheets and place on the pot pies.

Bake 10 to 12 minutes, or until the filo is golden. Serve at once.

Serves 4

ROMAINE, SPINACH, AND RED CABBAGE SALAD WITH CELERY SEED DRESSING

147
CALORIES PER SERVING

This beautiful salad is high in calcium, fiber, and vitamin C. These are sturdy vegetables, so the spinach and romaine can be washed and spun dry early in the day and stored in plastic bags in the refrigerator.

1 head of romaine
½ bunch spinach (about 6 ounces)
½ small head red cabbage

CELERY SEED DRESSING
¾ cup rice wine vinegar
2 tablespoons olive oil
1 tablespoon Dijon mustard
1 tablespoon grated onion
1 teaspoon fructose
1 tablespoon celery seeds

Separate the romaine leaves, wash them well, and spin dry. Tear the leaves into pieces and place in a salad bowl. Cut off and discard the spinach stems. Wash the spinach in several changes of water and spin dry. Tear the spinach into pieces and add to the romaine. Shred the cabbage coarsely and add to the greens.

To make the dressing, put the vinegar, oil, mustard, onion, fructose, and celery seeds in a small bowl and whisk to blend. Use 9 or 10 tablespoons of the dressing for the salad, and store the remaining dressing in a tightly covered jar in the refrigerator for up to 3 days.

Serves 4

SPA GINGERBREAD

132
CALORIES PER SERVING

The aroma of gingerbread baking is reward enough for the few minutes it takes to whip up the cake. Serve it warm, and add a dollop of Spa Whipped Cream if you're feeling indulgent.

¼ cup vegetable oil
½ cup molasses
¼ cup honey
2 cups whole wheat flour
1¼ teaspoons ground ginger
1 teaspoon ground cinnamon
½ teaspoon freshly grated nutmeg
1 teaspoon baking soda
1 large egg, beaten
½ cup buttermilk
Norwich Spa Whipped Cream (page 23) (optional)

Preheat the oven to 350° F. Spray a 9-inch-square baking pan with vegetable cooking spray and dust with whole wheat flour, shaking out the excess.

In a small saucepan, heat the oil, molasses, and honey just to a boil over moderate heat. Transfer the mixture to a large mixing bowl and let cool.

Sift together the flour, ginger, cinnamon, nutmeg, and baking soda.

Beat the egg into the molasses mixture, then beat in the flour mixture alternately with the buttermilk. Pour the batter into the pan and bake for 25 to 30 minutes, or until a cake tester or toothpick inserted in the center of the cake comes out clean. Let the cake cool on a rack until warm. Cut into 16 squares and serve with whipped cream, if desired.

Makes 16 squares

HARVEST

FEAST

BAKED OYSTERS
WITH
CRAB-WATERCRESS
BUTTER
•
TOURNEDOS
OF VENISON WITH
ROOT VEGETABLES
•
BRAISED KALE WITH
SHIITAKE MUSHROOMS
•
ACORN SQUASH
WITH MAPLE SYRUP
AND GINGER
•
PEAR TART
•

BAKED OYSTERS WITH CRAB-WATERCRESS BUTTER

104
CALORIES PER SERVING

This was one of the first recipes we developed at the Norwich Spa. It's our version of oysters Rockefeller, with fresh crab meat as the surprise ingredient.

½ cup (1 stick) unsalted butter, softened
½ cup buttermilk, or as needed
¼ cup chopped watercress
3 tablespoons chopped shallots
1 teaspoon minced garlic
1 cup crab meat, picked over and coarsely chopped
2 tablespoons fresh lime juice
Dash of hot pepper sauce
Vegetable seasoning
36 oysters in their shells

Cream the butter in a mixing bowl with an electric mixer. Gradually beat in ½ cup of buttermilk, adding more until the butter has doubled in volume. Add the watercress, shallots, garlic, crab meat, lime juice, hot pepper sauce, and vegetable seasoning to taste.

Transfer the butter mixture to a sheet of parchment or wax paper and form it into a cylinder about 1½ inches in diameter. Freeze the butter until firm, about 1 hour.

Preheat the oven to 350° F.

Open the oysters and discard the top shells. Sever the muscle from the lower shells, but leave the oysters in them. Arrange the oysters in a baking dish.

Cut the crab-watercress butter into 36 thin slices and place a slice over each oyster. Bake for 3 to 5 minutes, or just until the butter melts. Serve at once.

Serve 12

TOURNEDOS OF VENISON WITH ROOT VEGETABLES

250
CALORIES PER SERVING

Venison is not often found at city butchers or supermarkets, although it is beginning to be more widely available as more people realize how low in cholesterol and high in flavor it is. The loin of venison is a particularly tasty cut and, though comparatively tender, it benefits from the intensely flavored port wine and herb marinade. The veal stock used in the sauce should be rich and full-bodied.

4 pounds boned venison loin

MARINADE
½ cup port wine
1 cup red wine
2 garlic cloves
¼ cup juniper berries
1 bay leaf
3 or 4 fresh thyme sprigs
5 or 6 fresh sage leaves
2 tablespoons extra-virgin olive oil
2 or 3 grinds black pepper
Vegetable seasoning

2 small onions
1 small carrot, peeled
1 small celery stalk
1 parsnip, peeled
1 small turnip, peeled
1 tablespoon cold-pressed safflower oil
3 tablespoons whole wheat flour
1 cup coarsely chopped mushrooms
1 tablespoon tomato paste
1 quart Low-Sodium Veal Stock (page 143)
2 tablespoons red wine vinegar
1 cup fresh or frozen peas
4 to 6 sun-dried tomatoes (optional)

Ask your butcher to cut the venison into 12 cutlets of about 5 ounces each. In a bowl large enough to hold the venison, combine the port and red wine, garlic, juniper berries, bay leaf, thyme, sage, olive oil, black pepper, and vegetable seasoning to taste. Add the meat and stir to coat it with the marinade. Cover and refrigerate for at least 2 hours or overnight.

Preheat the oven to 350° F.

Cut the onions, carrot, celery, parsnip, and turnip into ¼-inch dice. Spray an 8-quart Dutch oven with vegetable cooking spray and add the oil. Place the casserole over moderately high heat and, when the oil is hot, add the onions, carrot, and celery. Sauté the vegetables until they begin to brown, 4 to 5 minutes. Transfer the vegetables to a plate and reserve.

Drain the venison, reserving 1 cup of the marinade, and pat dry with paper towels. Sprinkle the meat on both sides with the flour. Spray the casserole with vegetable cooking spray and place over moderately high heat. Add the venison and brown it in batches, about 5 minutes for each batch, turning the cutlets to brown on both sides and adding more vegetable cooking spray as necessary. Do not crowd the casserole or the venison will not brown properly.

Return all the venison to the Dutch oven, add the sautéed vegetables, diced parsnip and turnip, mushrooms, tomato paste, stock, reserved marinade, and vinegar. Bring the mixture to a boil, scraping up the browned bits at the bottom of the pan to incorporate them into the sauce. Cover the casserole and place it in the oven. Braise the venison for 30 minutes, skimming off excess fat 2 or 3 times during cooking.

Meanwhile, cook the peas in ½ cup of water for 2 to 3 minutes and drain.

Transfer the tournedos to a platter. Add the peas to the sauce, reheat if necessary, and spoon over the venison. Garnish with strips of sun-dried tomato, if desired.

Serves 12

BRAISED KALE WITH SHIITAKE MUSHROOMS

6 1

CALORIES PER SERVING

Kale's assertive flavor and distinctive texture are well matched here by the equally forthright shiitake mushrooms and sun-dried tomatoes.

2 pounds kale
10 ounces fresh shiitake mushrooms, or 4 ounces dried shiitakes reconstituted in 2 cups hot water and drained
14 to 16 sun-dried tomatoes, soaked for 2 minutes in boiling water and drained
2 teaspoons unsalted butter
2 medium onions, chopped
2 cups Low-Sodium Chicken Stock (page 141)
Vegetable seasoning
Freshly ground black pepper

Cut the kale leaves from the stalks, discarding the stalks. Wash the leaves carefully, because they tend to retain sand. Drain the kale and cut it into bite-size pieces.

Remove and discard the mushroom stems and slice the mushrooms into ¼-inch strips. Cut the tomatoes into slivers.

Place a large heavy saucepan over moderately low heat and spray with vegetable cooking spray. Add the butter and onions and sauté the onions until very lightly browned, about 5 minutes. Add the mushrooms and sauté 3 minutes. Add the kale and sauté until it has wilted a little, 4 to 5 minutes. Add the tomatoes and stock and bring to a boil. Reduce the heat and simmer, covered, about 10 minutes, removing the cover during the last 3 to 4 minutes of cooking to evaporate some of the juices. Add vegetable seasoning and pepper to taste.

Serves 12

ACORN SQUASH WITH MAPLE SYRUP AND GINGER

6 0

CALORIES PER SERVING

The lovely color and satisfying flavor of acorn squash are enhanced here by a hint of butter and maple syrup.

4 acorn squash (about 1 pound each)
1 tablespoon unsalted butter
2 tablespoons maple syrup
Scant ½ teaspoon ground ginger

Preheat the oven to 350° F. Cut the squash in half lengthwise and scoop out the seeds and membranes. Cut the pieces in half again and place them on a baking sheet. Bake the squash until tender, 40 to 50 minutes.

In a small saucepan, melt the butter. Add the maple syrup and ginger and swirl the pan to combine them. Spoon the syrup over the squash and serve at once.

Serves 12

PEAR TART

1 7 6

CALORIES PER SERVING

This inspired dessert is much faster and easier to make than you might think from looking at the recipe. Be sure the pears are very ripe and soft (but not mushy), or they won't be finished cooking when the pastry is done.

Whole Wheat Pastry (page 145)
1½ cups soft tofu
6 tablespoons honey
1 tablespoon vanilla extract
3 egg yolks
½ cup plus 1 tablespoon finely ground unblanched almonds
6 very ripe pears (Comice or Bartlett)
1½ cups fruit-only apricot jam

Preheat the oven to 350° F.

On a work surface dusted lightly with whole wheat flour roll half of the whole wheat pastry dough into a rectangle about ⅛ inch thick, 16 inches long, and 5½ to 6 inches wide. With a sharp knife, cut about 1 inch from each of the long sides of the rectangle, leaving a rectangle 4 inches wide and 16 inches long. Transfer to a 12 x 17-inch jelly roll pan.

Cut the 2 long scraps of dough into strips ¾ inch wide and 16 inches long. With a pastry brush, moisten the long edges of the rectangle and place the strips on them flush with the edges, pressing lightly to make them adhere. Repeat with the remaining dough.

Bake the shells for 8 to 10 minutes, or until they are firm, and let cool on the baking sheet. Leave the oven set at 350° F.

Place the tofu, honey, vanilla, egg yolks, and ground almonds in the bowl of a food processor fitted with the steel blade and process until the ingredients form a cream. Spread the cream evenly inside the cooled pastry shells.

Peel the pears and halve lengthwise. Cut out the cores and arrange 6 halves cut side down over the pastry cream on each tart. Bake the tarts for about 20 minutes, or until the crust is slightly brown and the pears are soft. Remove from the oven and let cool for about 5 to 7 minutes.

In a small saucepan, heat the jam over moderate heat until thinned out. Glaze the pears with the apricot jam, using a pastry brush. Chill the tart and serve cold.

Serves 12

C L A M B A K E

NEWPORT CLAM CHOWDER

·

COLESLAW, SLICED TOMATOES

·

NEW ENGLAND CLAMBAKE
STEAMED LOBSTER, MUSSELS,
HERBED FINNAN HADDIE

·

RED BLISS POTATOES,
CORN ON THE COB

·

SUMMER SHORTCAKES

·

NONALCOHOLIC BEER,
MINERAL WATER

·

NEWPORT CLAM CHOWDER

110
CALORIES PER SERVING

This absolutely delicious and altogether fatless chowder should be prepared at home early on the day of the clambake. For the tenderest results, the soup can be reheated and the clams added at the beach, as shown here. You might find it easier, though, to assemble the soup at home and transport it to the beach in vacuum flasks.

2 quarts littleneck clams
3 cups water
1 teaspoon chopped garlic
2 tablespoons chopped shallots
2 large onions, chopped
4 celery stalks, cut into ¼-inch dice
2½ cups peeled potatoes cut into
   ½-inch dice
½ cup dry sherry
2 or 3 bay leaves
   Pinch of ground mace
½ cup fresh lemon thyme leaves
   Vegetable seasoning
   Freshly ground white pepper

Scrub the clams under running water to remove all the sand. Place the clams, water, garlic, and shallots in a heavy pot, cover, and bring to a boil over high heat. Steam the clams until all of them are open, about 5 minutes; discard any that do not open. Remove the clams from their shells (you should have about 2 cups) and set aside. Strain the clam broth through cheesecloth or paper towels, measure the liquid, and add enough water to make 6 cups. Reserve.

Spray the bottom of a heavy saucepan with vegetable cooking spray and place the pan over moderately low heat. Add the onions and celery, cover the pan, and sauté the vegetables until they are transparent, stirring them

occasionally. Add the potatoes, reserved clam broth, sherry, bay leaves, and mace and bring to a boil over high heat. Reduce the heat, cover the pan, and simmer until the potatoes are tender, 15 to 20 minutes. The chowder can be prepared in advance to this point.

To serve, reheat the soup in the pot, add the reserved clams, thyme, and vegetable seasoning and pepper to taste, bring just to a boil, and serve at once.

Serves 8

COLESLAW

47
CALORIES PER SERVING

It's not a real clambake without coleslaw. Ours has cabbage, of course, plus carrots, scallions, apple, and a sweet and sour dressing. Prepare the salad at home and pack it in a tightly covered container.

6 cups shredded cabbage
1 cup shredded carrots
½ cup chopped scallions
1 tart apple, cored and chopped
1 tablespoon celery seeds
½ cup nonfat plain yogurt
2 tablespoons cider vinegar
1 tablespoon fructose
   Vegetable seasoning
   Freshly ground white pepper

In a large salad bowl, combine the cabbage, carrots, scallions, and apple and toss to mix. In a small bowl, combine the celery seeds, yogurt, vinegar, fructose, and vegetable seasoning and pepper to taste and blend well. Pour the dressing over the salad and toss until the ingredients are well mixed. Cover the coleslaw and allow the flavors to blend for 1 to 2 hours before serving.

Serves 8

NEW ENGLAND CLAMBAKE

433
CALORIES PER SERVING

Everyone has a great time at a clambake, and there's something for everyone to do. In fact, there's always so much work when you get to the beach that it's best to do most of the food preparation at home. In this recipe, the potatoes, onions, mussels, finnan haddie, and herbs should all be prepared early and packed in coolers with the corn, the lobsters, and the other dishes.

Remember to bring 8 large double pieces of cheesecloth, a pair of scissors, and kitchen twine or plastic twists. To make the fire, you'll need shovels, rakes, flat rocks, wood to build the fire, a half bushel of rockweed, and a large piece of canvas to cover the baking pit while the food cooks.

8 medium Red Bliss potatoes
2 large onions
8 whole cloves
3 dozen large mussels
1 to 1½ pounds finnan haddie
   (smoked cod fillets)
1½ teaspoons hot pepper flakes
¼ cup chopped fresh basil
¼ cup chopped fresh dill or
   fennel tops
¼ cup snipped chives
¼ cup chopped shallots
2 tablespoons minced garlic
8 small bay leaves
8 medium ears corn, husks on but
   silk removed
8 1-pound lobsters
4 to 6 large tomatoes, cored
   and sliced
   Basil leaves
   Malt vinegar
   Hot pepper sauce

At home, bring the potatoes to boil in a large pan of water over high heat and cook until tender, about 20 minutes. Drain and cool the potatoes. Cut the onions into quarters and stick a whole clove into each quarter. Scrub and debeard the mussels. Cut the finnan haddie into 8 pieces. In a small bowl, combine the pepper flakes, basil, dill, chives, shallots, and garlic, and cover the bowl tightly with plastic wrap.

At the beach, prepare a baking pit by digging a hole in the sand 6 to 12 inches deep and about 2 feet by 3 feet. Line the bottom of the pit with flat rocks and build a large fire on the rocks.

While the fire is heating up, assemble individual cheesecloth bags as follows: spread open a piece of cheesecloth on a flat surface and place a potato and an onion quarter in the center. Place 4 or 6 mussels around the potato and onion, and cover with a piece of finnan haddie. Sprinkle one-eighth of the herb mixture over each piece of fish. Top with a bay leaf and tie the bag with either kitchen twine or a plastic twist, leaving plenty of room for the mussels to steam open.

When the rocks are white hot, quickly layer them with 6 to 8 inches of rockweed. Spread the corn out over the seaweed, add 2 to 3 inches more of the rockweed, then make a layer of the lobsters and cheesecloth sacks. Wet the canvas thoroughly with seawater, cover the entire pit, and anchor it with strategically placed rocks. Bake the seafood and vegetables for 45 minutes to 1 hour.

Arrange the cooked lobsters, corn, and cheesecloth bags on plates. Add a few slices of tomato and decorate with basil leaves. Serve with malt vinegar and hot pepper sauce on the side.

Serves 8

SUMMER SHORTCAKES

1 5 7
CALORIES PER SERVING

The all-American summer dessert, these shortcakes are light and just sweet enough to satisfy your craving for sugar. The shortcakes can be made a week or so in advance and frozen until the day of the clambake.

SHORTCAKES
   2 large eggs
   4 egg whites
   ½ cup honey
   6 tablespoons whole wheat pastry flour
   6 tablespoons all-purpose flour

   1 quart mixed fresh berries (strawberries, raspberries, blueberries, blackberries)
   ½ cup fructose

VANILLA CREAM
   1 cup low-fat cottage cheese
   ½ cup nonfat plain yogurt
   1 tablespoon vanilla extract

To make the shortcakes, preheat the oven to 350° F. Line cupcake or muffin tins with paper liners, or spray the tins with vegetable cooking spray.

In a mixing bowl, beat the eggs, egg whites, and honey with an electric mixer until the mixture is thick and lemon-colored and ribbons form when the beaters are lifted from the bowl, about 5 to 7 minutes.

Sift together the flours, then fold the dry ingredients into the egg mixture,

taking care not to overmix. Spoon the batter into the prepared tins and bake for about 10 minutes, or until the shortcakes are lightly browned. Carefully remove the shortcakes from the tins and let cool on racks.

In a bowl, toss the berries with the fructose, blend well, and allow the juices to develop for 1 or 2 hours.

To make the vanilla cream, put the cottage cheese, yogurt, and vanilla in a blender and puree until smooth. Transfer the mixture to a serving bowl.

To serve, pass the shortcakes, fruit, and vanilla cream separately, and allow your guests to assemble their own desserts.

Makes 12 shortcakes

W I N T E R
T E A

BREAST OF CHICKEN
ROULADE
ON BROWN BREAD

•

ROLLED ASPARAGUS
SANDWICHES

•

CUCUMBER-DILL
TEA SANDWICHES

•

ARTICHOKE HEARTS
STUFFED WITH
CRABMEAT
(page 94)

•

CRANBERRY-OAT
TEA BREADS

•

WHOLE WHEAT SCONES
WITH FRESH APPLE
AND MINTED PEAR BUTTERS
(pages 18, 19)

•

MINIATURE
ZUCCHINI MUFFINS
(page 50)

•

INDIVIDUAL
CHEESECAKES

•

HERBAL TEAS

•

BREAST OF CHICKEN ROULADE ON BROWN BREAD

175
CALORIES PER SERVING

Leftovers are delicious for lunch or as an appetizer before dinner. They can be frozen, too, but not for more than a week.

- **2 boneless, skinless chicken breasts (10 ounces each)**
- **4 to 6 ounces boneless chicken meat (from the breast or thigh), cut into 1-inch pieces**
- **2 egg whites**
- **½ teaspoon minced garlic**
- **1 tablespoon minced shallot**
- **¼ cup finely chopped red bell pepper**
- **¼ cup finely chopped yellow bell pepper**
- **1 teaspoon chopped fresh oregano or ¼ teaspoon dried**
- **1 teaspoon snipped fresh chives**
- **1 teaspoon chopped fresh tarragon or ¼ teaspoon dried**
- **2 teaspoons chopped fresh chervil or ½ teaspoon dried**
- **1 teaspoon chopped fresh sage or ¼ teaspoon crumbled dried**
- **Vegetable seasoning**
- **Freshly ground white pepper**
- **16 thin slices pumpernickel bread**

CURRY SPREAD
- **1 tablespoon curry powder**
- **1½ teaspoons low-sodium soy sauce**
- **1 cup low-fat plain yogurt**
- **½ cup mashed soft tofu**

Trim all the fat from the chicken breasts, cut the breasts in half, and flatten them with a mallet or the flat side of a heavy knife. Set aside.

Place the additional chicken meat in the bowl of a food processor fitted with the steel blade. Add the egg whites and process until the mixture is smooth. Transfer it to a bowl and add the garlic, shallot, bell peppers, and herbs. Stir in vegetable seasoning and white pepper to taste and mix very well.

Spread the mixture evenly over the flattened chicken breasts and roll up each piece from a long end, jelly roll fashion. Wrap each roll tightly in 2 layers of plastic wrap. Place the rolls in the top of a steamer over boiling water and steam for 10 to 15 minutes. Let the chicken cool completely, then cut each roll into 8 slices.

Cut the bread into rounds the same size as the chicken slices.

To make the curry spread, combine the curry powder, soy sauce, yogurt, and tofu in a blender and puree.

Spread the bread with the curry puree, then top with a slice of chicken roulade and arrange on a serving plate.

Serves 8

ROLLED ASPARAGUS SANDWICHES

50
CALORIES PER SERVING

These are the sine qua non for a New England tea party. Be sure the bread is very fresh and fine-grained so it will roll easily around the asparagus.

- **16 asparagus spears**
- **4 thin slices whole wheat bread**
- **2 tablespoons unsalted butter, softened to room temperature**
- **2 teaspoons buttermilk or nonfat plain yogurt**
- **Pinch of grated lemon zest**
- **½ teaspoon fresh lemon juice**
- **Vegetable seasoning**
- **Freshly ground white pepper**

Trim the asparagus spears to 4-inch lengths (discard the bottoms or reserve for stock) and blanch for 2 minutes in boiling water. Drain the asparagus and place in a bowl of cold water to stop cooking and set the color.

Trim the crusts from the bread and gently flatten each slice with a rolling pin. Cut each slice into 2 triangles.

In a small bowl, cream together the butter, buttermilk, lemon zest and juice, and vegetable seasoning and pepper to taste. Spread this mixture evenly over the bread. Place 2 asparagus spears on each triangle of bread, tips toward the point of the triangle. Fold in the sides of each triangle at the base; the creamed butter mixture should be sufficient to hold the packages together. Chill the sandwiches before serving.

Serves 8

CUCUMBER-DILL TEA SANDWICHES

114
CALORIES PER SERVING

Serve these soon after they're assembled so the cucumber doesn't become limp and soggy.

- **¼ cup low-fat cream cheese**
- **¾ cup nonfat plain yogurt**
- **1 tablespoon chopped fresh dill**
- **1 teaspoon fresh lemon juice**
- **Vegetable seasoning**
- **Freshly ground white pepper**
- **4 slices whole-grain bread**
- **1 cup peeled thinly sliced European cucumbers**
- **Fresh dill sprigs**

In a bowl combine the cream cheese, yogurt, chopped dill, lemon juice, and vegetable seasoning and white pepper to taste and mix until well blended. Cut off and discard the crusts from the bread and spread each slice with the cheese mixture. Cut the sandwiches into triangles, rectangles, or circles and arrange the cucumber slices on top. Decorate with dill sprigs.

Serves 4

CRANBERRY-OAT TEA BREADS

64
CALORIES PER ½-INCH SLICE

This moist tea bread is baked in miniature loaf pans.

- ½ **navel orange**
- ½ **cup (1 stick) unsalted butter or margarine, softened**
- ¾ **cup packed dark brown sugar**
- 2 **egg whites**
- ½ **cup low-fat plain yogurt**
- ¼ **cup skim milk**
- 1½ **cups whole wheat pastry flour**
- 1 **teaspoon baking powder**
- 1 **teaspoon baking soda**
- ½ **teaspoon ground cinnamon**
- ½ **teaspoon ground cloves**
- 1 **cup rolled oats**
- 1 **cup chopped fresh or frozen cranberries**

Preheat the oven to 350° F. Spray four 3¼ x 5½ x 2-inch miniature loaf pans with vegetable cooking spray.

Cut the orange half into chunks and place in the bowl of a food processor fitted with the steel blade. Pulse the machine until the orange is ground. Transfer the orange to a mixing bowl, add the butter and sugar, and cream the mixture with an electric mixer or by hand. Beat in the egg whites. In a cup, stir the yogurt and milk to blend them, then add the mixture to the creamed ingredients and beat until well mixed.

Sift together the flour, baking powder, baking soda, cinnamon, and cloves into another mixing bowl, then stir in the oats. Fold the dry ingredients into the butter mixture, then fold in the cranberries.

Divide the batter among the loaf pans and bake for 50 to 60 minutes, or until they are firm and golden brown. Let the breads cool in the pans on racks. Unmold and slice the breads ½ inch thick.

Makes 4 loaves

WHOLE WHEAT SCONES

134
CALORIES PER SCONE

A fabulous British import, for tea or at breakfast, scones are an old-fashioned treat. Bake scones shortly before serving them, because they dry out within a few hours.

- 2 **cups whole wheat pastry flour**
- ¼ **cup wheat germ**
- 4 **teaspoons baking powder**
- ¼ **cup safflower oil**
- 2 **egg whites**
- ¾ **cup buttermilk**
- ¼ **cup raisins**
  Fresh Apple Butter and Minted Pear Butter (pages 18, 19)

Preheat the oven to 350° F.

In a mixing bowl, combine the flour, wheat germ, and baking powder and stir until well mixed. In another bowl, beat the oil, egg whites, and buttermilk until well blended. Add the buttermilk mixture slowly to the flour mixture, stirring to make a soft dough. Stir in the raisins, mixing just until they are well distributed. Turn the dough out onto a floured work surface and let it rest for 5 to 10 minutes.

Roll out the dough ½ inch thick, cut into 2-inch rounds, and arrange the scones on an ungreased baking sheet. Bake 15 to 20 minutes, or until the tops are golden brown. Serve hot with apple and minted pear butters.

Makes 1 dozen 2-inch scones

INDIVIDUAL CHEESECAKES

46
CALORIES PER CHEESECAKE

These cakes, made with low-fat cheeses, are relatively low in cholesterol and very high in protein and calcium. Our recipe makes about 32 small cakes, but fortunately they freeze very well.

- 1 **cup fresh whole wheat bread crumbs**
- 2 **tablespoons apple juice**
- 8 **ounces low-fat cream cheese, at room temperature**
- 8 **ounces part-skim ricotta cheese, at room temperature**
- ¼ **cup fructose**
- 1 **large egg**
- 2 **egg whites**
- 1 **teaspoon vanilla extract**

Preheat the oven to 350° F. Put paper liners in 32 miniature muffin tins.

Place the crumbs in a small bowl and stir in the apple juice to moisten. Sprinkle about 1 teaspoon of the crumb mixture in each muffin cup and bake for 3 to 5 minutes, or until golden brown. Set the muffin cups aside to cool. Leave the oven on.

Place the cream cheese and ricotta in a mixing bowl and cream with an electric mixer until soft and creamy. Add the fructose, egg, egg whites, and vanilla and beat until very well mixed. (The batter can also be mixed in a food processor.)

With a very large spoon, ladle about 4 teaspoons of batter into each muffin cup. Bake for 8 to 10 minutes, or until the cheesecakes are set and beginning to brown around the edges. Let cool and then chill the cakes.

To freeze leftovers, place the cheesecakes on a baking sheet and freeze. Transfer the cakes to plastic freezer bags and store for about 1 month.

Makes 32 miniature cheesecakes

F O R M A L

DOUBLE CONSOMMÉ
(page 141)
•
ROAST CAPON
•
APPLE CORN BREAD AND
WILD MUSHROOM DRESSING
•
BEETS WITH DILL AND
HORSERADISH SAUCE
•
SPINACH WITH GARLIC, OIL, AND
PIGNOLI NUTS
•
TREVISO AND FRISÉE SALAD
•
SALZBURGER NOCKERL
•

DINNER

ROAST CAPON

191

CALORIES PER SERVING

Capon is larger, meatier, and juicier than ordinary chicken and is a good choice for a holiday meal when a turkey is too large. Order the capon in advance from your butcher to be assured of a fresh, not frozen bird.

- 1 capon (8 to 9 pounds)
- Freshly ground white pepper
- Vegetable seasoning
- 1½ tablespoons cold-pressed safflower oil

Preheat the oven to 350° F.

Remove the giblets and neck from the cavity and wash the bird well inside and out; pat dry. Bend the wing tips back behind the shoulders. Season the cavity well with white pepper and vegetable seasoning. Cross the drumsticks over the tail and press the leg joints up into the bottom of the breast. Tie the drumsticks together at the tail with kitchen twine. Rub the oil all over the capon and season generously with white pepper and vegetable seasoning.

Place the bird in a roasting pan and roast, uncovered, for about 3½ hours, or until the thigh juices run clear when pierced with the tip of a knife. (A meat thermometer inserted into the inside of the thigh without touching the bone should register 185° F.) Tent the capon with foil if it browns too quickly.

Remove the pan from the oven, transfer the capon to a serving platter, and set aside the pan with its juices. Tent the capon with foil, if you haven't already done so, and let it stand for about 15 minutes while you make the gravy.

Serve in thin slices with the well-skimmed pan juices.

Serves 8

APPLE CORN BREAD AND WILD MUSHROOM DRESSING

275

CALORIES PER SERVING

Put the dressing in the oven 15 minutes before the capon is due to come out.

- 1 pound cultivated mushrooms
- 4 ounces fresh shiitake mushrooms, stems removed
- 4 ounces fresh oyster mushrooms
- 1 tablespoon unsalted butter
- 1 medium onion, coarsely chopped
- 1 celery stalk, cut into ¼-inch dice
- 1½ tablespoons chopped fresh sage
- Vegetable seasoning
- 1 recipe Apple Corn Bread, cubed
- 1 large egg
- ½ cup skim milk
- ½ to 1 cup Low-Sodium Chicken Stock (page 141)

Preheat the oven to 350° F. Spray a shallow 2-quart casserole with vegetable cooking spray. Coarsely chop the mushrooms and reserve.

Spray a large nonstick skillet with vegetable cooking spray, place over moderate heat, and add the butter. When the butter is melted, add the onion and sauté until translucent, about 5 minutes. Add the celery and sauté 3 minutes longer. Add the mushrooms and sage and toss to combine. Add vegetable seasoning to taste and set aside to cool.

In a large bowl combine the corn bread and add mushroom mixture and mix lightly. Whisk the egg and milk together, add to the corn bread mixture, toss and mix well. If the dressing seems dry, add chicken stock ¼ cup at a time.

Spoon the dressing into the casserole, cover with foil, and bake for about 30 minutes, or until it is set, removing the foil 10 minutes before the end of baking to brown the top.

Serves 8

APPLE CORN BREAD

109

CALORIES PER SERVING

- 2 cups skim milk
- 1 tablespoon rice wine vinegar
- 2 tablespoons unsalted butter
- 2 cups stone-ground yellow cornmeal
- 2 tablespoons fructose
- 1½ teaspoons vegetable seasoning
- 1 large egg
- 2 egg whites
- 1 teaspoon baking soda mixed with 1 tablespoon water
- 1 medium apple, cored and coarsely chopped

In a bowl, combine the milk and vinegar and let stand for 5 minutes.

Melt the butter in the top of a stainless-steel double boiler set over low heat. Remove the pan from the heat and add the cornmeal, fructose, vegetable seasoning, and soured milk and stir to mix well. Place the pan over a pot of boiling water and cook, stirring occasionally, until the mixture thickens, about 2 to 3 minutes. Transfer the cornmeal mixture to a mixing bowl and let cool.

Preheat the oven to 350° F. Spray a 9-inch-square baking dish with vegetable cooking spray, dust with whole wheat flour, and shake out the excess.

In a small bowl, beat the egg and egg whites to mix well. Add the eggs, dissolved baking soda, and apple to the cornmeal mixture and beat until well blended. Pour the batter into the pan and bake for 25 to 30 minutes, or until a toothpick inserted in the center of the corn bread comes out clean. Unmold the corn bread onto a rack and let cool.

Serves 16

BEETS WITH DILL AND HORSERADISH SAUCE

44
CALORIES PER SERVING

A pungent mixture of horseradish and yogurt adds zing to the sliced beets.

6 to 8 medium beets (about 2 pounds in all)
½ cup nonfat plain yogurt
1½ to 2 teaspoons prepared white horseradish (page 15)
2 tablespoons snipped fresh dill

Scrub, cook, and peel the beets (page 74). Cut them into ⅜-inch slices and keep them hot in the top of a double boiler set over simmering water.

In a small bowl, stir the yogurt, horseradish, and dill until blended.

When ready to serve, arrange the beets on serving plates and spoon a dollop of sauce over them.

Serves 8

SPINACH WITH GARLIC, OIL, AND PIGNOLI NUTS

47
CALORIES PER SERVING

Pignoli nuts are very rich in flavor, and in calories, too. Fortunately, even a few of them will impart a luxurious taste to sautéed spinach.

4 teaspoons pignoli nuts
2 pounds spinach
4 teaspoons extra-virgin olive oil
2 garlic cloves, minced
Freshly ground black pepper

Place the pignolis in a small dry skillet and toast them over moderate heat for 3 to 4 minutes, shaking the pan constantly, until the nuts are browned.

Trim off the root ends from the spinach, discard the stems if you like, and wash the leaves very well. Drain it in a colander, shaking out most of the water. Without adding more liquid, put the spinach in a large heavy saucepan, place over high heat, and cook, stirring and tossing, until just tender, about 4 or 5 minutes.

Meanwhile, in a small skillet or pan, heat the oil over moderately low heat, add the garlic, and cook for 1 or 2 minutes, just long enough to coat the garlic and mellow its raw taste; do not brown.

Drain the spinach, pressing out most of the moisture, and return it to the saucepan. Add the oil and garlic mixture and a generous grinding of black pepper and toss lightly. Sprinkle with the nuts and serve.

Serves 8

TREVISO AND FRISÉE SALAD

52
CALORIES PER SERVING

Treviso has long, narrow red leaves and belongs to the same family as radicchio, which you can use as a substitute.

Hazelnut Oil Dressing (page 38)
1 pound frisée
2 heads Treviso lettuce or radicchio

Wash the frisée and Treviso carefully. Spin dry and store in a plastic bag in the refrigerator until just before serving time.

To serve, arrange the lettuces on salad plates, whisk the dressing, and spoon it over the salad.

Serves 8

SALZBURGER NOCKERL

117
CALORIES PER SERVING

Gossamer light, our maple-syrup-flavored omelets are based on a famous Austrian dessert.

6 egg whites, at room temperature
⅓ cup plus 1 tablespoon fructose
¼ cup maple syrup
3 egg yolks
4½ tablespoons whole wheat pastry flour
¼ cup evaporated skim milk
1 tablespoon unsalted butter or margarine
1 cup fresh berries
Mint sprigs

Preheat the oven to 350° F.

In a large mixing bowl, beat the egg whites and fructose until soft peaks form. Gradually add the maple syrup, beating constantly until stiff peaks form. In a cup, lightly stir the egg yolks with a fork. Fold the egg yolks into the meringue. Sprinkle the meringue with the flour and fold it in.

Pour the milk into a large oval casserole, add the butter, and bake for 8 to 10 minutes, or until the milk is hot and the butter is melted. Drop 8 large spoonfuls of the egg mixture over the milk and bake 10 to 15 minutes, or until the omelets are browned. Transfer the nockerls to dessert plates, spooning some of the milk around each serving. Garnish with a few berries and a mint sprig.

Serves 8

fundamentals

BASIC SPA RECIPES

HERBED WHOLE WHEAT BREAD CRUMBS

7

CALORIES PER TABLESPOON

A good way to use stale bread, these bread crumbs can be stored in the freezer.

2 slices whole wheat bread
1 tablespoon dried basil
1 teaspoon dried thyme
1 tablespoon chopped fresh chervil
¼ teaspoon minced garlic
1 teaspoon minced shallots

Preheat the oven to 325° F. Spray a baking pan with vegetable cooking spray.

Tear the bread into pieces and place in the bowl of a food processor fitted with the steel blade. Add the seasonings and process until the bread is ground. Spread the crumbs on the baking sheet and toast for 8 to 10 minutes, or until dried. Cool and store in an airtight container.

Makes about 1 cup

SPA VINAIGRETTE

24

CALORIES PER TABLESPOON

We use this basic vinaigrette to dress every kind of salad, whether it contains greens, cooked or raw vegetables, or cooked fish. Add whatever herbs are appropriate for the salad; instead of lime juice, use orange, grapefruit, or lemon; grate citrus zest into the dressing— have fun with it. To cut the calories even further, omit the shallots and chives and put the dressing in a spray bottle to spritz onto a salad. Toss chives in afterward.

1 tablespoon Dijon or whole-grain mustard
2 tablespoons cold-pressed safflower oil or extra-virgin olive oil
2 tablespoons red or white wine vinegar
6 to 7 tablespoons mineral water
1½ teaspoons fresh lime juice
2 tablespoons chopped shallots
1 tablespoon snipped chives
½ teaspoon freshly grated white pepper
Vegetable seasoning

Put the mustard in a small bowl and slowly whisk in the oil. Whisk in the vinegar, mineral water, lime juice, shallots, chives, pepper, and vegetable seasoning to taste. Store in a tightly covered container in the refrigerator for up to 1 week.

Makes ¾ cup

LIGHT TOMATO SAUCE

100

CALORIES PER CUP

You'll find many ways to serve this delicious sauce. It has a clean, fresh flavor that complements other foods but doesn't drown their taste.

1 tablespoon extra-virgin olive oil
1 tablespoon minced garlic
½ cup chopped onions
1 small carrot, peeled and chopped (about ½ cup)
½ cup chopped celery
2 cups low-sodium canned tomatoes, undrained
1 tablespoon chopped fresh basil or 1 teaspoon dried
1 tablespoon chopped fresh oregano or 1 teaspoon dried
Vegetable seasoning
Freshly ground white pepper

Heat the oil in a heavy 1½-quart saucepan over moderate heat. Add the garlic, onions, carrot, and celery and sauté for 5 minutes, stirring often. Add the tomatoes, basil, and oregano and bring the mixture to a simmer. Reduce the heat, cover, and simmer the sauce for 1 hour.

Transfer the sauce to a food processor fitted with the steel blade and process briefly to make a slightly chunky sauce. Season to taste with vegetable seasoning and pepper.

Makes 3 cups

RED WINE TOMATO SAUCE

76

CALORIES PER CUP

Red wine adds depth to this easily prepared tomato sauce. Use it in dishes where its resonance will be matched by the flavors of other foods.

½ **cup dry red wine**
1 **medium onion, chopped**
2 **tablespoons minced garlic**
½ **cup chopped peeled carrots**
½ **cup chopped celery**
1 **quart low-sodium canned tomatoes, undrained**
2 **tablespoons chopped fresh basil or 1½ teaspoons dried**
2 **tablespoons fresh oregano or 1½ teaspoons dried**
Vegetable seasoning
Freshly ground white pepper

Pour the wine into a heavy 2-quart saucepan, add the onion and garlic, and bring to a simmer over moderately low heat. Cook the mixture, uncovered, for 5 minutes, then add the carrots and celery and simmer 5 minutes more. Add the tomatoes, basil, oregano, and vegetable seasoning and white pepper to taste and bring to a simmer over moderate heat. Reduce the heat, cover the pan, and simmer the sauce for 1 hour.

Transfer the sauce to a food processor fitted with the steel blade and process until smooth.

Makes 1 quart

LOW-SODIUM CHICKEN STOCK

40

CALORIES PER CUP

This is the basic stock we use in many of our soups, sauces, and stews. It's practical to freeze roast chicken carcasses and combine them with raw chicken parts, but only the freshest vegetables and herbs should be used in the stock.

There's a certain amount of inertia to overcome in making stock, but just remind yourself that the actual preparation and cooking time is really minimal —it's the *stock* that cooks for hours.

4 **pounds chicken necks and backs or whole fowl**
5 **quarts cold water**
1 **large onion**
2 **celery stalks**
2 **carrots, peeled**
1 **leek**
1 **garlic clove**
1 **medium bunch Italian parsley**
5 **or 6 fresh thyme sprigs**
1 **bay leaf**
1 **tablespoon black peppercorns**

Wash the chicken parts thoroughly and, if you are using a whole fowl, disjoint the bird. Place the chicken in a large stockpot, add the water, and bring to a boil over high heat. As the water nears a boil, skim off the foam as it forms.

Meanwhile, chop the onion, celery, and carrots. Trim off the root end of the leek and most of the green top.

Wash the leek well and chop it. Add the vegetables and garlic to the stock, return to a boil, then immediately reduce the heat. Simmer the stock slowly, uncovered, for 3 hours, skimming off the foam occasionally. Add the parsley, including the stems, thyme, bay leaf, and peppercorns, and simmer the stock for 1 hour longer.

Strain the stock into a bowl and cool it quickly by placing the bowl of stock in a larger bowl of ice water. Stir the stock until it cools, replacing the ice in the larger bowl as needed. Refrigerate the stock. When it is cold, remove any fat that has congealed on the surface.

Pour the stock into plastic containers and store in the freezer for up to 3 months.

Makes 3 quarts

DOUBLE CONSOMMÉ

80

CALORIES PER ½ CUP

Consommé is stock that has been reduced and then clarified. To make double consommé, the stock is further enriched with browned poultry and vegetables and more seasonings. Additional flavorings are added when the consommé is clarified. The result is a rich, clear soup—one of the most elegant you can serve, and one of the least caloric.

The procedure described below can be employed to make veal or duck double consommé. Simply substitute veal or duck bones and ground veal or duck meat for the chicken.

DOUBLE CONSOMMÉ

3 pounds chicken wings, backs, and necks
2 celery stalks
1 medium carrot, peeled
1 large onion, unpeeled
3 quarts Low-Sodium Chicken Stock
1 medium bunch Italian parsley
1 tablespoon black peppercorns
3 fresh thyme sprigs
2 cups cold water

CLARIFICATION

8 ounces boneless, skinless chicken
2 celery stalks
1 small carrot, peeled
1 large leek
1 medium tomato
6 egg whites
¾ cup Madeira wine
1 tablespoon fresh lemon juice
1 medium bunch Italian parsley
2 fresh thyme sprigs
1 tablespoon black peppercorns
1 bay leaf

Preheat the oven to 375° F.

For the consommé, wash and dry the chicken parts, place them in a shallow roasting pan, and roast them for about 45 minutes, turning the pieces occasionally.

Meanwhile, chop the celery and carrot. Add the onion, celery, and carrot to the chicken and continue roasting until they are well browned, about 25 to 30 minutes, stirring from time to time.

Transfer the chicken and vegetables to a large stockpot. Place the roasting pan over high heat on top of the stove and deglaze it with 1 cup or more of stock, scraping up all the browned bits from the bottom.

Pour the deglazing liquid and solids into the stockpot, add the remaining stock, the parsley, peppercorns, thyme, and cold water, and bring to a boil over high heat. Reduce the heat until the liquid barely simmers and cook, uncovered, until it is reduced to 1½ quarts, about 2½ to 3 hours. Strain the liquid into a mixing bowl and cool as for Low-Sodium Chicken Stock. Chill the consommé and remove any fat that congeals on the surface.

To clarify the consommé, remove any fat on the boneless chicken meat and grind the meat in a food processor. Chop the celery and carrot fine. Trim the bottom and most of the green part from the leek, wash it well, and chop it fine. Coarsely chop the tomato.

In a mixing bowl, whisk the egg whites until they are frothy, add the ground chicken and chopped vegetables, and stir until well mixed. Transfer the mixture to a large stockpot and stir in the cold consommé. Add the Madeira, lemon juice, parsley, thyme, peppercorns, and bay leaf and stir well.

Place the stockpot over moderately high heat and bring to a boil, stirring frequently until the egg whites coagulate and form a "raft." Lower the heat and cook the consommé at a low simmer, uncovered, for 45 to 60 minutes.

Place a strainer over a bowl and line the strainer with a double layer of cheesecloth moistened with cold water and wrung out. Carefully ladle the consommé into the strainer and discard the residue of egg whites and vegetables in the stockpot.

Use the consommé immediately, or cool and store in the refrigerator.

Serves 8

FISH STOCK

1 2

CALORIES PER QUART

Fish stock is the basis for a variety of fish soups and stews, among them our own Norwich Seafood Chowder (page 75). Of all the stocks, this is the one that requires the least advance preparation. Just be sure that the fish bones are fresh and do not come from fatty fish, which would make the stock too strong.

4 to 5 pounds bones and heads, from lean white fish
1 medium onion, quartered
1 celery stalk, roughly chopped
½ parsnip, peeled and roughly chopped
½ cup mushroom stems (optional)
½ bunch parsley stems
Juice of ¼ lemon
1½ teaspoons white peppercorns
½ cup dry white wine
3 quarts water

Ask your fishmonger to remove the gills from the fish heads. Rinse the heads and bones in several changes of cold water. Drain the bones and place them in a 5-quart soup pot with the onion, celery, parsnip, mushroom stems, if desired, parsley, lemon juice, peppercorns, wine, and water. Bring to a boil over high heat, then reduce the heat and simmer the stock for 45 to 60 minutes. Strain through a colander lined with dampened cheesecloth. Cool the stock and refrigerate or freeze.

Makes 2 quarts

LOW-SODIUM VEAL STOCK

25
CALORIES PER CUP

In making veal stock, the bones are first browned in the oven to enrich the flavor and color of the stock. If you don't have a stockpot large enough to accommodate all the ingredients, use 2 pots or cut the recipe in half.

Veal stock can be transformed into double consommé, as described in the preceding recipe. To make a veal glaze (glace de viande), simmer 4 cups of the stock, uncovered, over very low heat until reduced to a few tablespoons. The glaze is a superb flavoring for soups and sauces.

10 pounds veal bones
1 cup dry red wine
4 Spanish onions
2 medium carrots, peeled
2 celery stalks
3 or 4 tomatoes, or 1 1-pound can
    low-sodium tomatoes, drained
1 medium bunch Italian parsley
10 to 12 fresh thyme sprigs
3 bay leaves
¼ cup black peppercorns

Ask your butcher to cut the bones into 1½-inch pieces.

Preheat the oven to 400° F.

Place the bones in a shallow roasting pan and roast until browned, about 45 to 60 minutes, turning once or twice.

Transfer the bones to a 3-gallon stockpot and add enough cold water to cover them by 2 inches. Place the roasting pan on top of the stove over high heat, pour in the wine, and deglaze the pan, stirring up the browned bits and juices at the bottom with a wooden spoon. Pour the deglazing liquid and solids into the stockpot and place over high heat. Bring the stock to a boil, frequently skimming off the foam as it forms on the surface of the liquid. Veal bones create a lot of foam and other impurities, so the stock should be skimmed quite often during the early cooking stages. Reduce the heat and simmer the stock, uncovered, slowly for 4½ to 5 hours, skimming as needed.

Cut the onions into quarters, cut the carrots and celery into 1-inch pieces, and coarsely chop the tomatoes. Add them, along with the parsley, thyme, bay leaves, and peppercorns, to the stock and simmer 1½ to 2 hours longer. Strain the stock into a mixing bowl, discarding the solids. Cool and store as described on page 141.

Makes 3 quarts

RICH VEAL STOCK

In a heavy saucepan, bring 3 quarts of veal stock to a boil over high heat. Lower the heat and simmer the stock, uncovered, very slowly until it is reduced to 1 quart.

HIGH-POTASSIUM VEGETABLE STOCK

28
CALORIES PER CUP

As part of our regular Spa program, we serve one vegetarian meal a day, and this robust stock is the basis for many of the soups and sauces on that menu. It's axiomatic that a stock whose flavor depends entirely on vegetables must be made with top-grade ingredients.

2 leeks
1 or 2 red or green bell peppers
3 carrots, peeled
2 or 3 onions
3 or 4 celery stalks
4 garlic cloves
1 or 2 zucchini or yellow squash
4 medium tomatoes
½ head green cabbage, or
    ½ bunch broccoli
½ medium bunch Italian parsley
4 fresh thyme sprigs
4 fresh basil, rosemary, or
    oregano sprigs
2 bay leaves
10 black peppercorns

Trim off the root end and most of the green part of the leeks, wash very well, and chop them coarsely. Core, seed, and coarsely chop the bell pepper. Roughly chop the carrots, onions, celery, garlic, zucchini, tomatoes, cabbage, and parsley. Place the vegetables in a large stockpot and cover with cold water; you'll need about 1 gallon.

Place the pot over high heat and bring to a boil. Add the thyme, basil, bay leaves, and peppercorns, reduce the heat, and simmer the stock, uncovered, for 1½ hours, skimming as needed.

Strain the stock into a bowl and cool to room temperature. Chill the stock and freeze it in plastic containers.

Makes 3 quarts

VARIATION: HIGH-POTASSIUM COUNTRY VEGETABLE SOUP

57
CALORIES PER SERVING

To 5 cups of High-Potassium Vegetable Stock, add a diced carrot, celery stalk, and parsnip. Simmer until the vegetables are tender, about 5 minutes. Serve with chopped scallion and a dash of vegetable seasoning.

SPA BÉCHAMEL

95

CALORIES PER ½ CUP

This recipe might serve as an exemplar of Yankee Ingenuity. The formula has been set on its ear, cholesterol has been eliminated, calories have been reduced, and the calcium content—the only conceivable nutritional benefit from ordinary béchamel—has been boosted.

Use Spa Béchamel the way you would regular white sauce, and add other herbs, spices, and seasonings to suit the food being sauced.

3 tablespoons nonfat dry milk powder
2 cups skim milk
2 tablespoons grated onion
2 tablespoons grated celery
2 tablespoons grated carrot
  Pinch of dried thyme
  Pinch of freshly grated nutmeg
  Pinch of freshly ground white
  pepper
1 bay leaf
2 tablespoons arrowroot mixed with
  2 tablespoons cold water

Put the dry milk powder in a heavy 1-quart saucepan and slowly stir in the milk. Add the onion, celery, carrot, thyme, nutmeg, white pepper, and bay leaf and bring to a boil over moderate heat. Reduce the heat until the sauce is barely simmering and cook, uncovered, for 20 minutes. Stir in the arrowroot mixture and, stirring constantly, cook 1 minute longer, or until the sauce has thickened. Strain through a fine-mesh strainer and adjust the seasoning.

Makes 1½ cups

SPA WHITE WINE SAUCE

131

CALORIES PER ½ CUP

Unlike our Spa béchamel, this sauce *is* thickened with a roux. Add herbs and seasoning toward the end of cooking, and use sparingly as you would béchamel.

2 cups dry white wine
2 tablespoons finely chopped shallots
1½ quarts skim milk
6 tablespoons margarine
½ cup all-purpose or whole wheat flour
1 bay leaf
  Freshly grated nutmeg

In a small saucepan over high heat, cook the wine and shallots until the wine is reduced by half, about 10 minutes. In a medium saucepan, scald the milk.

In another medium saucepan, melt the margarine over moderately low heat. Stir in the flour and cook the roux, stirring constantly, for 2 to 3 minutes, or until the flour is cooked but not colored. Whisk in the scalded milk and the wine mixture and bring to a boil, whisking constantly until the sauce is thickened. Add the bay leaf, reduce the heat, and cook the sauce at a very slow simmer for 20 minutes. Add nutmeg to taste and strain the sauce.

Makes 1½ quarts

WHOLE WHEAT PIZZA CRUSTS

125

CALORIES
PER 2½- TO
3-INCH CRUST

250

CALORIES
PER 6-INCH CRUST

This is a delicious high-fiber crust that's easy to make by hand and even easier if you use a food processor. The individual crusts are partially baked before being topped with any of the combinations on page 50 or any topping you choose. If you process the dough, bear in mind that the machine tends to heat ingredients slightly as it processes them, so use water that is at room temperature instead of lukewarm.

1¼ cups lukewarm water
2 packages active dry yeast
  (see Note)
2 teaspoons honey
¼ cup cold-pressed safflower oil
1 teaspoon sea salt
2½ cups whole wheat flour
¾ to 1 cup soy flour

To make the dough by hand, pour the water into a mixing bowl, add the yeast, and stir until dissolved. Stir in the honey, oil, salt, and flours and mix with a large spoon until a dough forms. Scrape the dough out onto a lightly floured surface and knead until smooth and elastic, about 5 to 8 minutes, dusting your hands with a little flour if necessary to keep the dough from sticking. The dough should not be too stiff.

To make the dough in a food processor, pour the room-temperature water into a 2-cup measure, stir in the yeast to dissolve it, and add the honey and oil. Place the salt and flours in the bowl of a food processor fitted with the steel blade. Pulse the mixture 3 times to combine well. With the motor running, pour the yeast mixture through the feed tube. Continue processing for about 40 seconds, or until the dough forms a ball around the shaft of the processor. If the dough is very sticky, add whole wheat flour 1 tablespoon at a time; if too dry, add water 1 teaspoon at a time. Turn the dough out onto a floured surface and knead by hand for 3 or 4 turns.

Form the dough into a ball and place in a lightly oiled bowl, turning to film the surface with oil. Cover the bowl and let the dough rest in a warm place until it has risen about 50 percent in bulk, about 45 to 60 minutes.

(If you do not wish to make the pizzas at once, wrap the dough in plastic wrap and refrigerate until you are ready to form the crusts.)

Preheat the oven to 400° F.

Punch down the dough, transfer it to a lightly floured surface, and cut into 16 walnut-size pieces. Form each piece into a ball about 1½ inches in diameter, then roll or stretch it by hand into a circle ⅛ to ¼ inch thick and 2½ to 3 inches in diameter. (If you prefer, cut the dough into 8 pieces and roll them into circles about 6 inches in diameter.) Spray lightly with vegetable cooking spray.

Arrange the circles, oiled side down, on baking sheets and let stand for 5 minutes (10 minutes if the dough is still cold from the refrigerator). Don't let the crusts stand around for long or they will balloon during baking.

Partially bake the crusts for 5 minutes. Add a topping immediately and bake until done, following individual topping instructions.

Makes sixteen 2½- to 3-inch pizza crusts or six 8-inch crusts

NOTE: We have not given the usual instructions for proofing the yeast before adding the other ingredients because all yeast, whether purchased in a supermarket or a health-food store, is marked with an expiration date, which, if heeded, guarantees that the yeast will work.

WHOLE WHEAT PASTRY DOUGH

3 1 8

CALORIES PER SERVING

This is a versatile pastry dough. The recipe makes enough for 2 tarts, but half can be frozen for later use.

3 cups whole wheat pastry flour
4½ teaspoons fructose
1½ cups (3 sticks) margarine, chilled
3 egg whites

In a large mixing bowl, combine the flour and fructose, mixing well with a fork. Cut each stick of margarine into 8 pieces, add to the flour mixture, and cut in with a pastry blender or 2 knives until the margarine is the size of small peas. In a small bowl, whisk the egg whites until frothy, then stir into the flour mixture with a fork to form a dough. Do not overmix or the dough will toughen. Form the dough into a rectangle, wrap in wax paper, and refrigerate until using, at least 1 hour.

VANILLA ICE CREAM

9 4

CALORIES PER SERVING

Our ice cream, made with a ricotta and cottage cheese base, is adapted from a Sicilian frozen dessert. Even without heavy cream, this is incredibly rich and satisfying. Although the ice cream will be delicious if made with vanilla extract, for a real big vanilla flavor use a vanilla bean.

1 cup skim milk
1 4- to 5-inch vanilla bean or
1 tablespoon vanilla extract
1 cup part-skim ricotta cheese
1 cup 1% fat cottage cheese
¼ cup fructose

In a small saucepan, scald the milk with the vanilla bean. (If you are using vanilla extract, do not add it yet.) Let the mixture cool, then slit open the vanilla bean with the tip of a small sharp knife and scrape the seeds into the milk.

Pour the milk into the bowl of a food processor fitted with the steel blade, add the ricotta, cottage cheese, fructose, and vanilla extract if using, and process until the mixture is perfectly smooth. Transfer to a bowl, cover, and chill in the refrigerator for up to 24 hours.

Freeze the mixture in an electric or hand-cranked ice-cream maker, following the manufacturer's instructions.

Makes 1 quart, serving 8

THE SPA PANTRY

One of the advantages of New Spa Food is that it is based on using fresh food in season, so you won't have to set aside miles of shelf space to accommodate the items in the list that follows.

We do, however, use some specialized products to add flavor without adding fats, sodium, or calories to our dishes. It is well worth your while to stock your pantry with our Spa Staples so you won't be tempted to resort to sodium-laden seasoned salts, cholesterol-rich creams and butters, or sugary sweeteners when preparing food for yourself and your family.

In fact, after you look over the list, there may be a few foods in your pantry now that you'd like to jettison on the road to healthy eating: caloric bottled salad dressings and mayonnaise; foods high in saturated fats, such as cottonseed, palm, and coconut oils, solid vegetable shortening, and lard; high-sodium soy sauce; dry cereals with added sugar; any packaged foods with emulsifiers and stabilizers such as xanthan and guar gums and carrageenan (often found in low-fat cottage cheese, ice creams, and sauces); and anything containing artificial colors, artificial flavors, or any preservatives whose safety you have reason to doubt.

It's heartening to see how many Spa pantry items that once could be purchased only in health-food stores are now readily available on supermarket shelves. A few are not, however, and you may have to seek them out in a health-food store, or shops specializing in Middle Eastern, Oriental, or Italian foods. (If you would find it more convenient to shop for some Spa pantry foods by mail, consult the mail order directory on page 149.)

The decision about whether to buy a food packaged or loose—whole wheat flour and other grain products come to mind—is a personal one, depending on convenience, how much of an item you need at the moment, how soon you'll be using whatever is left over, and cost. Many grains are fresher and less expensive when purchased loose, especially from a high-traffic health-food store. If you are unsure of how to cook a particular grain, you might want to buy it in a package the first time and save the cooking instructions to use later. Loose grains can be stored for long periods in airtight containers at room temperature.

FLOUR AND GRAINS

Whole wheat flour, which is used in many of our baked goods and in some of our sauces, is the Spa equivalent of unbleached all-purpose white flour. It's stocked in all supermarkets and can be bought loose in health-food stores. Stone-ground flour can be found in some supermarkets, but flour milled from organically grown wheat can be bought only in health-food stores. **Whole wheat pastry flour** contains less gluten than regular whole wheat flour and is used in Spa cakes because it produces a more delicate texture. The pastry flour is at present available mostly in health-food stores or from mail order sources.

There appears to be an infinite number of delicious **whole-grain breads** in every supermarket, and better ones still at farmers' markets and organic bakeries. Look for multigrain breads containing crunchy seeds and millet. Read the label of packaged bread before you buy it; most breads contain some sugar to give the yeast a boost, but if the sugar is very near the top of the ingredients list, the bread contains far too much of it. If you don't plan to use it within a day or two, store sliced bread in the freezer and toast it 1 or 2 slices at a time.

Quick-cooking couscous, which can almost be considered a convenience food, and **bulgur,** another grain product, are widely available in supermarkets, health-food stores, and Middle Eastern food stores.

Basmati rice, a delicate, fluffy, and aromatic long-grain rice, is the premier rice in India, where it originated. Recently basmati hybrids have been developed in the United States—white and brown varieties in Texas and a red basmati, sometimes called wahine, in California. The Texas-grown Texmatis, which can be bought in many supermarkets as well as in specialty and health-food stores, are delicious. If you think ordinary brown rice tastes heavy and somewhat flavorless, try brown basmati rice; its delicate texture and nutty flavor will win you over for life. Red basmati has its own unique and wonderful qualities: it tastes and smells similar to popcorn. Gourmet food shops and health-food stores are the best source for red basmati.

Kashi, the Breakfast Pilaf is the trade name of a combination of grains and seeds available in all supermarkets. It cooks up into a crunchy mixture that we serve hot or cold and use in salads or as an accompaniment to fish and poultry.

Soba noodles, Japanese pasta made of buckwheat flour or a combination of whole wheat and buckwheat, are available in some supermarkets and in all Oriental and health-food stores. **Whole wheat pasta,** some of it even imported from Italy, has found its way onto a number of supermarket shelves as well. Experiment with different pasta shapes, such as shells, penne, and fusilli.

SWEETENERS

Fructose is the sweetener of choice in New Spa Food. It's a natural component of sucrose (ordinary table sugar), but has twice the sweetening power and, therefore, half the calories of sucrose. By grinding fructose with a mortar and pestle, you can produce a sweet, fluffy powder very similar to confectioners' sugar. We generally avoid artificial sweeteners altogether, and because **honey** has high caloric content it is used only in those recipes where its pronounced flavor is desirable. Among the other natural sweeteners, New England's own **maple syrup** has such an unmistakable taste that just a little will sweeten and enhance desserts, hot cereals, and acorn squash, and **unsweetened apple juice** performs miracles as a sweetening agent in drinks, desserts, sauces, and even soups.

OILS AND FATS

Since the New Spa Food program strictly limits the amount of oil and fat in its recipes, you might as well get the best nutrition and flavor value from those you do use. In terms of nutrition, your healthiest choices are oils containing high proportions of monounsaturated and polyunsaturated fatty acids in comparison to saturated fatty acids, since mono- and polyunsaturated fats tend to lower serum cholesterol.

Cold-pressed extra-virgin olive oil (from the first pressing), a primarily monounsaturated fat, is so tasty that just a teaspoon or two of it can flavor a dish. The oil is generally imported from Europe, and it can be bought in a wide range of qualities, colors, and prices. Some very palatable brands are sold in supermarkets and some very exquisite vintage oils are sold in fancy food stores. Unless you are sure of the flavor of a particular oil, buy only a small amount to see if it suits your taste and the food it's used with. You might want to have several kinds on hand.

Most vegetable oils are rich in polyunsaturated fats; in almost all our recipes, we use **cold-pressed safflower oil, soy oil,** and **corn oil** in preference to saturated vegetable fats (some margarines and solid shortenings) and animal fats (butter and lard). It's important to read food package labels carefully; if such highly saturated fats as palm, cottonseed, and coconut oil appear in the ingredients list, don't buy that product.

Vegetable cooking spray, used alone or in combination with oil or butter, is often sprayed over a nonstick skillet and used for sautéing. There is also an olive-oil flavored vegetable cooking spray available, which you might want to use for Mediterranean dishes.

VINEGARS

At the Spa we use vinegar as a calorically inexpensive way of adding interest to fruits, soups, and stews and for deglazing sauté pans, as well as for salad dressings and pickling. In addition to good-quality **red wine** and **white wine vinegar,** your Spa pantry should include **balsamic vinegar,** delicious with fruits and for deglazing pans in which vegetables or meats have been sautéed; **raspberry vinegar,** which tastes good with fruit and adds a subtle sweetness to shredded vegetables; and **blueberry vinegar**—try a few drops of it on ice cream. Mild **rice wine vinegar** is wonderful for dressing greens and for adding a delicate acidity to sauces.

DRIED MUSHROOMS

Mushrooms add earthy flavor and depth to a variety of dishes, but few calories.

A number of mushrooms formerly found only in the wild are now being cultivated on mushroom farms, where they are called "exotic" mushrooms. **Shiitakes** and **oyster mushrooms** are two exotic ones, and they are sold fresh or dried in some supermarkets. Dried **Oriental black mushrooms,** very similar to shiitakes, are available in specialty food shops and all Oriental food stores. Mushrooms that are, as yet, uncultivated, such as **morels, cèpes, porcini,** and **Polish boletus,** can be bought dried in gourmet food shops. Although quite expensive, dried mushrooms offer good value; they're so flavorful that you'll need only a few of them to perfume grains, soups, vegetables, stews, and sauces, and the liquid in which they are reconstituted can be used in the same recipes or saved for stock. Stored in plastic bags in a cool dry place, dried mushrooms will keep for a very long time.

TOMATOES

Low-sodium canned tomatoes contain no added salt (tomatoes are naturally high in sodium). **Sun-dried tomatoes,** either from California or imported from Europe, add an intense tomatoey flavor to savory dishes. Use them sparingly, because they can easily overwhelm other flavors. Sun-dried tomatoes from California tend to be less salty and less leathery when reconstituted; several brands can be found in supermarkets.

SEASONINGS

We use **vegetable seasoning** much as you would salt, to boost natural flavors. A variety of salt-free seasoning mixtures made of dried herbs and vegetables, spices, and citrus rind can be bought in supermarkets and health-food stores. Some combinations are all-purpose, others are spicy, and so on. Whichever ones you buy, be sure they contain no MSG.

Black, white, red, and **green peppercorns** add punch and pungency to a wide range of dishes. Black and white peppercorns from various parts of East India are sold loose and packaged at supermarkets and gourmet food stores.

Green peppercorns, usually packed in brine, and red peppercorns can be found at specialty food shops. **Szechuan peppercorns,** sold in their husks, are available mostly in Oriental food stores. Dried peppercorns keep indefinitely.

Low-sodium soy sauce, as the name implies, has a lower sodium content than regular soy, and a milder flavor as well.

We hope you'll be able to find all the fresh herbs called for in our recipes, but it's inevitable that at some point one or more of them will be unavailable. In such a case, we suggest substituting another fresh herb—dill, Italian parsley, or chopped scallion tops, for instance—before using a dried herb. However, there are a number of dried herbs that are excellent, if used with discernment: sage, oregano, rosemary, and thyme work very well in some meat dishes and sauces. Write the date you open the jar on the label and discard it after 6 months, by which time the herb will have lost most of its flavor.

BEVERAGES

Weight-conscious people tend to quaff large quantities of diet soda, but there are many healthier *and* tastier alternatives. Still and sparkling **mineral** and **spring waters** and **sodium-free seltzer** quench the thirst, refresh the palate, cleanse the system, and have absolutely no calories.

100 percent fruit juices, plain or in a spritzer, are tasty options. Most of those on supermarket shelves are just what they should be—made from the fruit only. Some "nectars," however, contain high-fructose syrups and other additives, and some vegetable cocktails contain MSG, so look at the label carefully before you buy, and consider shopping for your juices in health-food stores.

At the Norwich Inn and Spa, we offer caffeine-free **herbal** and **fruit teas** with every meal. Keep several kinds on your pantry shelf so there'll always be one to suit your mood.

Regular and **espresso coffee** beans

that have been decaffeinated by a water process are available in many specialty food shops and supermarkets. You can have the coffee ground to suit your coffee maker or grind them yourself just before you brew the coffee. Store both beans and ground coffee in airtight containers in the freezer, where the beans will stay fresh for up to one year.

A number of the domestic and imported **nonalcoholic malt liquors** (less than 0.5 percent alcohol by volume) are quite convincing in flavor, and, at about 49 to 68 calories for 12 ounces, all of them are less caloric than even "lite" beer. If you have a few extra calories to spare, it might be fun to have a malt liquor tasting to see which of them you like best.

DAIRY PRODUCTS

Among dairy products, **evaporated skim milk** is one of our Spa staples. It's far less caloric than ordinary evaporated milk and very high in calcium. We use it extensively in cream sauces, custards, soups, and baked goods. **Nonfat dry milk powder** is used to increase the calcium in several dishes, especially in Spa Whipped Cream and some baked goods.

Although not strictly pantry items, **skim milk, nonfat yogurt,** and **low-fat ricotta** are all mainstays of New Spa Food. Check the labels to see that you're getting exactly what you want; that is, a purely dairy product, with no additives. This procedure becomes more problematic with low-fat cottage cheeses, many of which contain xanthan or carob gums and artificial flavors. At the Spa, we scan cottage cheese labels with an eagle eye. A mixture of low-fat ricotta and nonfat yogurt tastes similar to cottage cheese, but of course in no way approximates its texture.

Asiago is an Italian cheese similar to Parmesan (the only possible substitute for Asiago), but milder, less grainy, and less expensive. Asiago—ask

for aged cheese—is available in Italian food stores and at the cheese counters of some department store food sections (see Mail Order Sources, page 149).

COOKING EQUIPMENT

You won't need a duck press or a salamander to make New Spa Food, but there are a few utensils that should be part of your batterie de cuisine.

Nonstick skillets in 2 or 3 sizes (8, 10, and 12 inches in diameter) are wonderful for everything from making a single omelet to sautéing large quantities of chopped vegetables without the need for lots of oil or butter.

Nonstick muffin tins also make baking easier, allowing muffins to pop out without greasing the tins and adding unnecessary fat and calories.

A **cast-iron stove-top grill** with raised ridges and troughs, although not essential, is a utensil some people swear by. Its advantages are that while the raised ridges sear the food in an attractive pattern, the fat drains into the troughs, a most efficient way of cooking.

By now the **food processor** is regulation kitchen equipment. In addition to the 3 standard blades, a fine shredder and a julienne blade can be put to good use.

A **blender** is more effective than a processor for making frothy drinks, but should you be faced with the choice of purchasing only one of them, the processor wins hands down.

A **mini processor** will become indispensable once you begin using it to emulsify sauces, chop 1 pepper or 1 onion, and slice small amounts of vegetables.

Finally, an electric or hand-cranked **ice-cream maker** will bring joy to the life of any and all who prepare and eat New Spa Food. This quite inexpensive piece of machinery is easy for kids to operate, and there's nothing like homemade sorbet or ice cream to finish off a satisfying meal.

MAIL ORDER SOURCES

If you are unable to locate some of the specialty foods and products used in New Spa Food, you can order many of them from the mail order sources listed below. Call for catalog or price list before placing your order to learn about seasonal specials or sample-size products you may want to try.

Apple Pie Farm, Inc.
Union Hill Road, R.D. 5
Malvern, PA 19355
(215) 933-4215
• *fresh and dried herbs, flavored vinegars*

Baldwin Hill Bakery
Baldwin Hill Road
Phillipston, MA 01331
(508) 249-4691
• *fresh-baked whole-grain bread*

Barclay's Coffee & Tea Co.
9030 Tampa Ave.
Northridge, CA 91324
(818) 885-7744
• *water-decaffeinated coffee beans*

Bear Meadow Farm
Rte. 2, Moore Road
Florida, MA 01247
(413) 663-9241
• *herb and flavored vinegars*

Birkett Mills
Penn Yan, NY 14527
(315) 536-3311
• *stone-ground flours*

Broadmoor Baker
P.O. Box 24327
Seattle, WA 98124
(206) 329-3000, (800) 272-7323
• *fresh whole-grain bread*

Brown & Jenkins Trading Co.
P.O. Box 1570
Burlington, VT 05402-1570
(802) 862-2395, (800) 456-JAVA
• *water-decaffeinated coffee*

Butternut Mountain Farm
Johnson, VT 05656
(802) 635-7483
• *Vermont maple syrup*

Chef's Choice
65 Westover Drive
Asheville, NC 28801
(704) 255-0249
• *specialty and baking flours*

Corti Brothers
5770 Freeport Blvd., #66
Sacramento, CA 94822
(916) 391-0300
• *imported oils, gourmet items, and seasonings*

De Wildt Imports
R.D. 3
Bangor, PA 18013
(215) 588-0600, (800) 338-3433
• *brown and basmati rice, couscous, noodles*

Dimpflmeier Medieval Bread
69 Charles St.
New York, NY 10014
(212) 924-5718
• *homey hearth-baked bread*

Estus Gourmet
1499 67th St.
Emeryville, CA 94608
(415) 653-0496
• *rice of every description*

Farms of Texas Co.
P.O. Box 1305
Alvin, TX 77512
(713) 331-6481, (800) 232-RICE
• *Texas-grown basmati rice*

Festive Foods of Virginia, Inc.
20 Carrollton Road
Sterling, VA 22170-9949
(703) 450-4504
• *vinegars, dried mushrooms*

Fox Hill Farm
444 W. Michigan Ave., Box 79
Parma, MI 49269-0009
(517) 531-3179
• *fresh and dried herbs, herbal teas*

Genovesi Food Co.
P.O. Box 5668
Dayton, OH 45405
(513) 277-2173
• *imported sun-dried tomatoes*

Gillies Coffee Co.
160 Bleecker St.
New York, NY 10012
(212) 260-2130
• *coffee, herbal teas*

Green Mountain Sugar House
R.F.D. 1
Ludlow, VT 05149
(802) 228-7151
• *Vermont maple syrup*

Herb Gathering, Inc.
5742 Kenwood
Kansas City, MO 64110-2732
(816) 523-2653
• *fresh and dried herbs*

House of Spices
76-17 Broadway
Jackson Heights, NY 11373
(718) 476-1577
• *sun-dried tomatoes,*
vegetable seasoning, spices

Howard's Happy Honeybees
4828 Morro Drive
Bakersfield, CA 93307
(805) 366-4962
• *flavored honeys*

International Epicure, Inc.
17 Magret Terrace
Sparta, NJ 07871
(800) 622-3344
• *dried mushrooms*

Katagiri & Co., Inc.
224 E. 59th St.
New York, NY 10022
(212) 755-3566
• *Oriental vinegars,*
dried mushrooms, noodles

Kimberly Wine Vinegar Works
P.O. Box 40, Hunters Point
San Francisco, CA 94124
(415) 822-5850
• *fine wine vinegars*

Le Gourmand
Box 422, Rte. 22
Peru, NY 12972
(518) 643-2499
• *imported olive oils*

Meadowbrook Herb Gardens
R.R. Box 138
Wyoming, RI 02898
(401) 539-7603
• *peppercorns, dried herbs*
and seasonings

Mr. Spiceman
615 Palmer Road
Yonkers, NY 10701
(914) 961-7776
• *dried herbs and seasonings,*
peppercorns

My Cup of Tea
P.O. Box 946
Pasadena, CA 91102-0946
(800) 552-9463
• *herbal teas and specialty coffee*

Rafal Spice Co.
2521 Russell St.
Detroit, MI 48207
(313) 259-6373
• *peppercorns, seasoning mixtures, spices*

G. B. Ratto & Co. International Grocers
821 Washington St.
Oakland, CA 94607
(415) 832-6503, (800) 325-3483
• *flours, rice, bulgur, couscous, oils,*
sun-dried tomatoes

Select Origins
Box N
Southampton, NY 11968
(516) 288-1382, (800) 822-2092
• *rice, oils, vinegars, dried mushrooms*

Stash Tea Co.
P.O. Box 90
Portland, OR 97207
(503) 684-7944, (800) 826-4218
• *flavored herbal teas*

Sultan's Delight
P.O. Box 140253, 25 Croton Ave.
Staten Island, NY 10314-0014
(718) 720-1557
• *bulgur, couscous, grains*

Timber Crest Farms
4791 Dry Creek Road
Healdburg, CA 95448
(707) 433-8251
• *domestic sun-dried tomatoes*

United Society of Shakers
Sabbathday Lake
Poland Spring, ME 04274
(207) 926-4391
• *flavored vinegars, herbs, seeds*

Vanilla Saffron Imports, Inc.
70 Manchester St.
San Francisco, CA 94110
(415) 648-8990
• *herbs, dried mushrooms, peppercorns*

Walnut Acres
Penns Creek, PA 17862
(717) 837-0601
• *stone-ground flours, exotic rice, oils*

War Eagle Mill
Rte. 5   Rogers, AR 72756
(501) 789-5343
• *stone-ground flours*

a c k n o w l e d g m e n t s

Many people offered valuable assistance in the making of this book, and we would like to offer our heartfelt thanks to them all.

The talented people at Clarkson N. Potter made the process of putting this book together go so smoothly: Martha Schueneman, Ann Cahn, Teresa Nicholas, Howard Klein, Barbara Marks, and Carol Southern all played crucial roles. Special thanks go to Pam Krauss, our editor, a knowledgeable, gentle, encouraging presence throughout the entire project.

Our sincere gratitude goes also to our amazing photographic team: Maria Robledo, whose talent, unerring eye, and unfailing ability to see only the positive in every situation were priceless to us; we consider ourselves very lucky to have had the opportunity to work with her. Anita Calero, our very talented stylist, amazed us with her eccentric yet elegant eye for the unusual and made each photograph distinctive and unexpected. John Massie accomplished his very difficult job with grace, getting up at dawn to prepare, transport and then style every dish in the book with a naturalness that perfectly captured the spirit of our cooking philosophy. Roscoe Betsill also did yeoman's duty at the eleventh hour. Maria's very special assistants, Ann Faison, Debra Goldman, and Sandy Goines worked tirelessly; Daniel Kucharsky, the Spa's chef, worked with me to create many of the Spa recipes, cheerfully devising new dishes up to the very last minute; and lastly, thanks to Judy Knipe, whose contributions to the menus and text went far beyond what was required of her.

Special thanks also to Dania Martinez Davey, whose sensitive design gave the book its handsome look, and to Gael Towey, for her helpful suggestions. Regina Safdie, of Regina Linens in San Francisco, lent us many wonderful props. Peter Buse, President of the Edward J. Safdie Group, ensured that things ran smoothly at the Inn during our days of shooting, and Pia Carlstrom offered invaluable assistance in the clerical department. And our appreciation goes also to the entire staff at the Norwich Inn and Spa, who graciously tolerated our disruptive presence, doing everything they could to make our jobs easier.

And finally, to the following people living in southeastern Connecticut who were so kind and accommodating in allowing us to disrupt their lives for the time it took (during all four seasons!) to photograph this book, our gratitude:

Adrienne Tytla, of All Outdoors in East Lyme, whose beautiful grounds and antique garden furniture provided us with dozens of wonderful locations that made our job a pleasure;

John and Ann Adams, of Les Trois Provinces in Colchester, whose beautiful historic home and French country antiques grace many of our photographs;

Mr. Hader, who graciously allowed us to photograph on his lovely Stonington waterfront.

credits

THE SPA PROGRAM

DAY 1
Breakfast: Celadon bowl, plate, cup, and saucer, Ceralene Raynaud at Baccarat; silver and teapot, Thaxton & Co.; celadon dish, vase, and cloth, Vito Giallo Antiques
Lunch: Gravy boat, Henri Bendel; white salad plate, Thaxton & Co.; silver, Vito Giallo Antiques
Dinner: Plates, napkins, and vase, Henri Bendel; celadon candle holder, Vito Giallo Antiques

DAY 2
Breakfast: Bowl and saucer, Ceralene Raynaud at Baccarat; teacup, saucer, toast plate, and silver, Thaxton & Co.
Lunch: Plates, soup bowl, Ceralene Raynaud at Baccarat; glasses, Baccarat
Dinner: Plates, Cardel; glasses, Baccarat; dessert plate, Ceralene Raynaud at Baccarat

DAY 3
Breakfast: Silver, Vito Giallo Antiques; teapot, Thaxton & Co.
Lunch: Plates, Ceralene Raynaud at Baccarat
Dinner: Plates and candle holders, Cardel; glasses, Baccarat; silver, Thaxton; dessert plate and silk cloth, Vito Giallo Antiques

DAY 4
Breakfast: Creamer, plate, cup, and saucer, Cardell; tray, Henri Bendel; silver, Thaxton & Co.
Lunch: Plate, Cardell; cloth and napkin, Anichini; spoon, Vito Giallo Antiques
Dinner: Plates, dessert underplate, Ceralene Raynaud at Baccarat; napkins and cloth, Trouvaille Francais; candle holder, Thaxton & Co; glasses, Baccarat

DAY 5
Breakfast: Napkins, plates, tray, mugs, cutting board, Henri Bendel; spoons, vase, and small celadon bowl, Vito Giallo Antiques; glasses, Cardell
Lunch: Napkins, plate, soup plate, dessert serving bowl, Henri Bendel; sauce bowl, Luna Garcia at Henri Bendel; glasses and vase, Thaxton & Co.; footed bowls, Baccarat; serving spoon, Vito Giallo Antiques
Dinner: Plate, underplate, and dessert plate, Ceralene Raynaud at Baccarat; pitcher, candle holder, and glasses, Baccarat; blue vase, New Glass; tablecloth and napkins, Trouvaille Francais; footed glass bowl, Cardell; spoon, Thaxton & Co.

SNACKS
Green glass bowl, Vito Giallo Antiques; pitcher, Henri Bendel; blue pitcher, Gallery Nielsson New Glass; glassware, Baccarat; tablecloth and runner, Trouvaille Francais

YANKEE INGENUITY

DAY 1
Breakfast: Coffeepot, plates, and glassware, Baccarat; silverware, Thaxton & Co.; spoon (in drink), Vito Giallo Antiques; pitcher, Gallery Nielsson New Glass
Lunch: Sauce bowls, Vito Giallo Antiques; tablecloth, Trouvaille Francais; plate, Thaxton & Co.
Dinner: plates, dessert plates, Limoges from Thaxton & Co.; candlesticks, Baccarat; vase, Henri Bendel; cloth and napkins, Vito Giallo Antiques

DAY 2
Breakfast: Bowl and plates, Ceralene Raynaud at Baccarat; silver, Vito Giallo Antiques
Lunch: soup bowl and plates, Luna Garcia at Henri Bendel; silverware, Vito Giallo Antiques; cloth, Anichini
Dinner: Soup plate, Thaxton & Co.; tablecloth, Trouvaille Francais; beer glass, New Glass; plate, Henri Bendel

DAY 3
Breakfast: Coffeepot, cup, and saucers, Baccarat; plates with fruit, Thaxton & Co.; small celadon bowl, vase, and green glass bowl, Vito Giallo Antiques; napkins, Henri Bendel; cloth, Trouvaille Francais
Lunch: Plates, Ceralene Raynaud at Baccarat; tablecloth, Trouvaille Francais; birdcage, Vito Giallo Antiques; footed crystal bowl, Baccarat
Dinner: Platter, Thaxton & Co.; napkin and tablecloth, Vito Giallo Antiques; plate and glasses, Baccarat; dessert glass bowl, Cardell; plate, Ceralene Raynaud at Baccarat

DAY 4
Breakfast: plates, pitcher, teacups, Thaxton & Co.; napkins, Henri Bendel; glass creamer, Henri Bendel
Lunch: Cloth, Vito Giallo; plate and glasses, Baccarat; dessert spoon, Thaxton & Co.

DAY 5
Breakfast: Napkins, mugs, and bowls, Henri Bendel
Lunch: Napkins and plates, Henri Bendel; silverware, Thaxton & Co.; vase and small bowl, Vito Giallo Antiques; glassware, Cardell
Dinner: Plates, Cardell; cloth, Trouvaille Francais; footed dessert dish, Baccarat; silver pitcher and candlesticks, Vito Giallo Antiques

SPECIAL SOUPS
Flower bowls, flower patterned lip bowl, glass bowl, Baccarat

MORE SPA DESSERTS
Celadon plates, strawberry roll platter, Baccarat; Tablecloth and napkin, Anichini; Apple spice cake platter and tray with peaches, Thaxton & Co.

SPECIAL OCCASIONS

BRUNCH
Pitcher and glassware, Gallery Nielsson New Glass; plates, soup bowls, Umbrello; napkin (with cookies), Henri Bendel; napkins and tablecloth, Trouvaille Francais

OPEN HOUSE
Meat platter, Thaxton & Co.; glassware, plates, and other servers, Baccarat; pitcher and glass bowl, Henri Bendel; runner, Trouvaille Francais; copper bowl and silverware, Vito Giallo Antiques

CLAMBAKE
Tablecloth, Vito Giallo Antiques; fruit platter and nutcracker, Baccarat

WINTER TEA
Plate with scones, back plate and saucers, Cardell; front plate with cup and saucer, Thaxton & Co.; napkins, Trouvaille Francais

TAILGATE PICNIC
Serving plate, picnic basket, tablecloth, and napkins, Vito Giallo Antiques

HARVEST FEAST
Plates, oyster plate, Limoges at Thaxton & Co.; glassware, Baccarat; silver salad bowl, Cardell; sterling platter, water pitcher, Thaxton and Co.; tablecloth, Vito Giallo Antiques

APRÈS SKI
Plates, soup bowls, and gravy boat, Cardell; napkins and tablecloth, Trouvaille Francais; glassware, Baccarat; silverware and candle holders, Vito Giallo Antiques; sterling silver pitcher and serving tray, Thaxton & Co.; wood tray, Henri Bendel; soup terrine, Baccarat

FORMAL WINTER DINNER
Soup plate and underplate, Tiffany; sterling silverware and candle holders, Georg Jensen at Royal Copenhagen; glassware, meat platter, Baccarat

JACKET

Antique Steuben vase, Vito Giallo Antiques; silver, Georg Jensen at Royal Copenhagen; plate, Wolfman, Gold

Index